trotman

Choosing your A levels and post-16 options

2nd Edition

Gary Woodward

For Mum, Dad and Daniel

Choosing your A levels and post-16 options
Second edition

This second edition published in 2006 by Trotman and Company Limited
2 The Green, Richmond, Surrey TW9 1PL

© Trotman and Company Limited, 2006

Editorial and Publishing Team
Author Gary Woodward
Editorial Mina Patria, Editorial Director; Jo Jacomb, Editorial Manager;
Catherine Travers, Managing Editor; Ian Turner, Editorial Assistant
Production Ken Ruskin, Head of Manufacturing and Logistics; James
Rudge, Production Artworker
Sales and Marketing Suzanne Johnson, Marketing Manager
Advertising Tom Lee, Commercial Director

Cover design by XAB
Text design by James Rudge

British Library Cataloguing in Publication Data
A catalogue record for this book is available from the British Library

ISBN 1 84455 102 4

Typeset by Photoprint, Torquay
Printed and bound by Creative Print & Design Group (Wales) Ltd.

Contents

About the author

Gary Woodward is a qualified careers consultant and freelance careers writer. He has written numerous articles for careers magazines and websites, as well as for national newspapers on a wide range of topics. He has significant experience of advising young people on job-hunting strategies as well as helping more experienced professionals with their career development. He is also author of the book *Winning Job-hunting Strategies for First-time Job-hunters.*

Acknowledgements

Thanks to Neil Roscoe for sharing his insights about A levels and A level teaching.

Introduction

What next? This is a question that you will probably ask yourself at many points in your life, but it's a question that's especially important when you're thinking about your post-16 qualifications, education or occupations. You may be thinking of taking A levels or a similar qualification and this book gives you details of the most popular ones so you can make the most informed choice. The kinds of questions this book can help you answer include:

- What A levels are available?
- What are the other post-16 options?
- How can I choose between different A levels?
- Which A levels do I need to study certain university subjects?
- How can I study and revise effectively?
- What do I learn in specific subjects?
- How do subject choices affect my career?

While the main focus here is on A levels and AS levels, there is also information about A level equivalents such as Scottish Highers, the International Baccalaureate, the Welsh Baccalaureate and others. Whatever your situation, getting the right answers to the questions listed above is very important: snap decisions at this stage can have significant consequences later on in life. Hopefully, though, with the aid of this book, you will be able to navigate your way successfully through the qualifications maze and make the best choices for you. I wish you well in your journey.

How to use this book

Part One of this book focuses on the different post-16 options available to you. Part Two is a directory of A level and AS level subjects. The final part discusses how to make your studies a success and includes information on how exam boards assess A level work, with some hints and tips about studying and revising effectively. The end note explores some of the options open to you after your post-16 qualification. If you're not sure of the meaning of the terms used in the book, you can refer to the glossary of terms and abbreviations on page 4.

You may already have realised from your experience of studying so far that everybody learns in a different way. In the same way, people read books differently. Some like to read them cover to cover; others prefer to start with the section that is most relevant to them. You can approach this book in either way. If you need a complete introduction to A levels and their equivalents, it would be a good idea to read through the book sequentially and make a note of any especially important points. If you already have some knowledge but need help with a specific issue, then the following questionnaire should be able to point you to the most relevant areas:

	A level (or equivalent) issue	Which section of the book?
1	I want to do further study after my GCSEs (or equivalent), but I'm not sure whether A levels are the best option.	See 'What are the options?' and 'Choosing your qualification' in Part One, pages 9 and 16
2	I need to find out about the different kinds of post-16 qualification.	See 'What are the options?' and 'Choosing your qualification' in Part One, pages 9 and 16
3	I can't decide on my third A level choice. How can I choose between two subjects I really enjoy?	See 'Choosing your subjects' in Part One, page 24
4	I know what I want to study at university but I'm not sure which A levels I should choose.	See 'Choosing your subjects' in Part One, page 24; and Part Two
5	I want to improve my effectiveness at studying, revision and taking exams.	See 'Making a success of your studies' in Part Three, page 241
6	I want to find out details about each A level and AS level subject.	See Part Two
7	I want to go straight into work after my post-16 qualifications.	See 'Choosing your qualification' in Part One, page 16; Part Two ('non-graduate jobs' section for relevant subjects); and 'End note: What next?' in Part Three, page 248
8	I want to find out about A level equivalents such as Scottish Highers, IB and BTEC, and apprenticeships.	See 'What are the options?' and 'Choosing your qualification' in Part One, pages 9 and 16
9	I want to find out which qualification is best for certain types of work or further study.	See 'Choosing your qualification' in Part One, page 16
10	I want some ideas about what to do after my post-16 qualification.	See 'End note: What next?' in Part Three, page 248

Glossary of terms and abbreviations

Term/abbreviation	Definition
A level	Advanced level
AEA	Advanced Extension Awards. These are for candidates who want to reach an exceptionally high standard in their subjects
ACCAC	Qualifications, Curriculum and Assessment Authority for Wales
Applied A levels	GCE A levels in vocational areas
Apprenticeships	A way for young people to train while working in particular skilled areas
AQA	Assessment and Qualifications Alliance. One of the three main exam boards in the UK
AS level	Advanced Subsidiary level. Forms half of a full A level, but is also a qualification in its own right
A2	Advanced level – the second half of a full A level
BA	Bachelor of Arts degree
BEd	Bachelor of Education degree
BEng	Bachelor of Engineering degree
BMus	Bachelor of Music degree
BSc	Bachelor of Science degree
CCEA	Council for Curriculum Education and Assessment (Exam Board in Northern Ireland)
Diploma	Usually lasts one or two years and is often related to a specific area of work. Can be taken after a Level 3 qualification or at postgraduate level
Edexcel	One of the three main exam boards in England
FdA	Foundation degree (Arts)

FdSc	Foundation degree (Science)
Fieldwork/Field trip	Practical activities related to a subject of study that take place away from school or college, often outdoors, such as a visit to a site of archaeological importance
Foundation course	A one-year programme designed to give students the necessary knowledge in a subject to prepare them for higher education. Most common for Art and Design where students need extra time to prepare a portfolio of work to enable them to get into higher education
Foundation degree	This lasts two years part-time and is a combination of study and work experience. Can be converted to an Honours degree or used to go on to specific areas of employment
Gap year	A year out, often taken between school and university or between graduation and starting a career
GCE	General Certificate of Education
HND	Higher National Diploma
IB	International Baccalaureate
NVQ	National Vocational Qualifications
OCR	Oxford, Cambridge and Royal Society of Arts Examining Board
PGCE	Postgraduate Certificate in Education (a requirement for most trainee teachers)
QCA	Qualifications and Curriculum Authority
Sandwich course	A degree course that includes a year of work
Syllabus	An outline of the course of study produced by exam boards. More recently called a specification
SQA	Scottish Qualifications Authority
Synoptic	This forms part of any A level qualification. It means that students have to make connections across the different units they've learned to show a broad understanding of the subject
UCAS	Universities and Colleges Admissions Service. This is the central body for handling applications to universities. You can also search for courses on their website
WBQ	Welsh Baccalaureate Qualification

PART ONE: OPTIONS AND DECISIONS

What are the options?

This section covers:
» *an outline of the most popular post-16 qualification and training options.*

There is no doubt that the more qualifications you have, the easier it is to get into certain types of work. For some people it is taken as read that after their GCSEs they will go on to do A levels, but have you ever stopped to ask yourself any of the following questions:

» Am I good at studying?
» Do I enjoy studying?
» Have my results been good enough to warrant further study?
» Do I need to study further for the kind of job I want to do?
» Do I understand the degree of difficulty and volume of work that may be associated with further study?

If you've answered 'no' to one or more of these questions, then it's probably worth taking some time to weigh up all the options before going ahead. The most popular options, including A levels, are outlined below.

GCE A levels and AS levels

A levels are probably the most widely known post-16 qualification and they are still seen as the traditional gateway to higher education. In the past, A levels consisted of a two-year course with exams at the end. In September 2000, the 16–19 education system was changed to encourage more breadth of knowledge and learning, and now the A level consists of two parts: the AS and the A2.

The Advanced Subsidiary (AS) is a stand-alone qualification and is valued as half a full A level qualification. It consists of three units (assessed at the standard expected for a student half way through an A level course), which contribute 50% of the full A level. The A2 is the second half of a full A level qualification. It also has three units (assessed at the standard expected for a student at the end of a full A level course), which contribute the remaining 50% of the full A level qualification. Most units are assessed by examination. Some are assessed by coursework. In most A levels, coursework accounts for 20 to 30% of the marks.

The AS covers the less demanding material in an A level course, and the A2 covers the more demanding material. For example, in the A2, students might:

» Specialise in an area they studied at AS
» Extend their knowledge and understanding of the subject by studying new topics
» Improve their skills.

Also in the A2, students will combine knowledge, understanding and skills from across the A level course. AS levels and A levels are still the most traditionally academic qualifications for 16–19 year olds. Trials are currently underway to test new ways of challenging the most able students using additional optional questions and a new extended project. A reduction in the number of assessments for each subject (from six to four) is also under consideration and changes may be introduced by September 2008.

GCE A levels in Applied Subjects
These types of A levels replace VCE A levels. The new qualifications give students a broad introduction to a vocational area and may use different methods of assessment compared to traditional A levels, such as case studies and work-related portfolios. At the time of going to press, the qualifications are available at both AS and A level in the following ten subject areas:

» Applied Art and Design
» Applied Business
» Applied ICT
» Applied Science
» Engineering
» Health and Social Care
» Leisure Studies
» Media: Communication and Production
» Performing Arts
» Travel and Tourism.

Key Skills
With the changes in the post-16 education sector has come a greater emphasis on developing skills as well as acquiring knowledge. Key Skills

are now part of the new National Qualifications Framework (NQF). The most important skills that have been identified for everybody to have are:

- » **Communication.** Reading, writing, speaking and listening. These are important not just for courses in modern languages, but for all subjects.
- » **Application of number.** Acquiring the ability to use numbers, graphs and data in a variety of contexts and for a variety of purposes. It's not just about doing calculations, but about showing that you have numerical reasoning ability.
- » **Information Technology (ICT).** Using hardware and software in different ways for different purposes. Most subjects now use ICT or computing to a greater or lesser extent, as do the vast majority of jobs.
- » **Working with others.** This is about being an active and responsible team member and learning to relate to others in a group situation effectively.
- » **Improving one's own learning and performance.** This involves self-development and recognising strengths and weaknesses, a crucial aspect of personal and career development.
- » **Problem solving.** The ability to analyse situations and generate creative solutions to solve problems.

Three of these skills – communication, application of number, and information technology – are available as a qualification. Schools and colleges vary a lot in terms of whether they offer this option to students: some do, some don't. Equally, many higher-education institutions, particularly the most traditional ones, may not accept this as counting towards your points tally for entry onto a degree course.

AEAs (Advanced Extension Awards)
AEAs are designed to challenge the most able A level students, ensuring that they are tested against standards comparable with the most demanding found in other countries. They are designed to be accessible to all able students, whatever their school or college and whichever specification they are studying. They will also help universities differentiate between the most able candidates, particularly in subjects with a high proportion of A grades at A level.

International Baccalaureate (IB)
This programme was born out of efforts to establish a common curriculum and university entry credential for students moving from one country to another. It was thought that students should share an academic experience that would emphasise critical thinking, intercultural

understanding and exposure to a variety of points of view. The programme has earned a reputation for rigorous assessment, giving IB diploma holders access to the world's leading universities. The programme is a comprehensive two-year international curriculum available in English, French and Spanish.

Apprenticeships

Apprentices learn on the job, building up knowledge and skills, gaining qualifications and earning money all at the same time. There are different levels of Apprenticeship available, but they all lead to one of the following:

» National Vocational Qualifications (NVQs)
» Key Skills qualifications
» A technical certificate such as a BTEC or City & Guilds.

Apprenticeships are increasingly popular and are a good way to further your career plans, but they're not for everyone. In return for good training and qualifications, apprentices have to apply those skills to the best job possible. The kind of subjects potential apprentices can take include:

» Administration
» Agriculture
» Construction
» Customer Service, Retailing and Wholesaling
» Engineering
» Finance, Insurance and Real Estate
» Health and Beauty
» Manufacturing
» Media and Printing
» Recreation and Travel
» Transportation.

National Vocational Qualifications (NVQs)

NVQs are work-related, competence-based qualifications. They reflect the skills and knowledge needed to do a job effectively, and show that a candidate is competent in a particular area of work. NVQs are based on national occupational standards. These standards are statements of performance that describe what competent people in a particular occupation are expected to be able to do. NVQs are achieved through assessment and training. Assessment is normally through on-the-job observation and questioning. Candidates produce evidence to prove they have the competence to meet the NVQ standards. Assessors sign off units when the candidates are ready. The assessor tests candidates' knowledge, understanding and work-based performance to make sure they can demonstrate competence in the workplace.

OCR Nationals
OCR Nationals are designed to cater for those who want to develop skills and knowledge through work-related learning. They provide candidates with high-quality, industry-recognised certificates, geared to vocational-sector requirements. Targeted primarily at post-16 learners, OCR Nationals will ultimately be available at Levels 1–3 of the National Qualifications Framework (see page 16). OCR Nationals can be delivered through flexible study programmes – either full time or part time – alongside other qualifications. Students can earn different amounts of UCAS points depending on the level studied and standard achieved.

BTEC (Business Technology and Education Council) qualifications
These could be a BTEC First (one-year course) or a BTEC National Diploma (two-year course). The BTEC First can be used to help you get into training or employment or to move on to the next stage of study (BTEC Diploma, AVCE or other options). The BTEC Diploma can also be used to get into training or employment, but since it is an equivalent to A levels it can also lead to higher education.

Scottish Highers
The Scottish Higher qualification is taken in S5 and S6 (Years 12 and 13). It can lead to a job or entry to further and higher education. While A levels are taken over two years, it only takes one year to study for a Higher. Therefore it's common to take between four and six Highers in any one academic year. Like A levels, Highers have been revamped recently to improve the choice available to students. The new Highers provide a broader range of options for progression beyond the Scottish Standard Grade level. There are five levels:

» Access
» Intermediate 1
» Intermediate 2
» Higher
» Advanced Higher.

Having five levels means that there will be more scope to demonstrate your abilities at a level that's right for you. Each level is designed to encourage you to move on to the next. Each qualification consists of three units, including an exam for all levels at Intermediate 1 and above.

Each unit is a qualification in its own right (called National Units). There is an exam in May/June on everything you have covered in the course, which will be combined with your coursework to give you a final grade. A full list of subjects that can be studied is on the Scottish Qualifications Authority website (www.sqa.org.uk), but here are the main ones:

- Accounting and Finance
- Administration
- Applied Mathematics
- Art and Design
- Biology
- Biotechnology
- Business Management
- Care
- Chemistry
- Classical Greek
- Classical Studies
- Communication and Media
- Computing
- Construction
- Contemporary Social Studies
- Craft and Design
- Dance
- Drama
- Economics
- Electronics
- Engineering
- French
- Gaelic

- Geography
- German
- History
- Information Systems
- Italian
- Mathematics
- Media Studies
- Music
- Philosophy
- Physical Education
- Physics
- Politics
- Product Design
- Psychology
- Religious Studies
- Russian
- Science
- Sociology
- Spanish
- Sport and Leisure
- Travel and Tourism
- Latin
- Urdu.

Welsh Baccalaureate

The Welsh Baccalaureate aims to create a broad, diverse study curriculum for students aged 16 to 18. Instead of taking three subjects, WBQ students first study core, practical options on contemporary Welsh life – for example Employment and European Awareness. Optional subjects can then be picked from courses already on offer through A levels and other qualifications. The emphasis is on work and industrial experience and the argument is that this system will better prepare students for university or the workplace.

CACHE Diploma

CACHE stands for the Council for Awards in Childcare and Education. This is one of the main bodies that awards qualifications at different levels for those who want to specialise in working with children. The organisation offers diplomas at different levels and attracts points on the UCAS tariff, the system that calculates entry points for university.

Diploma in Foundation Studies
The primary aim of the Level 3 Diploma in Foundation Studies (Art and Design) is to educate students to make informed decisions that will help their progression to appropriate higher education in art and design. It builds on the students' prior experience and skills and comprises nine units, all of which are mandatory. These units are in three stages. There are three units in the first stage, four in the second stage and two in the final stage. This staged structure supports the progressive development of the student towards independent and self-reliant learning.

How to find out more about each type of qualification

- A levels and AS levels – see Part Two of this book
- International Baccalaureate – www.ibo.org
- Apprenticeships – www.apprenticeships.org.uk
  www.scottish-enterprise.com/modernapprenticeships
- NVQs – www.dfes.gov.uk/nvq
- BTEC – www.btec.org.uk
- OCR Nationals – www.ocr.org.uk; www.ucas.com
- Scottish Highers – www.sqa.org.uk
- Welsh Baccalaureate – www.wbq.org.uk
- CACHE Diploma – www.dfes.gov.uk; www.qca.org.uk
- Diploma in Foundation Studies – www.edexcel.org.uk.

By now you should have an idea of some of the most common post-16 options, but how do you decide between them? The next chapter will help.

Choosing your qualification

In this section you will:
- » *get help with choosing the right post-16 qualification*
- » *learn about the UCAS tariff*
- » *find out how the different qualifications compare to one another in terms of academic level*
- » *do a brief exercise to help you choose the right qualification.*

With so many different options it can be a bit overwhelming, so how do you go about making the best choice? One of the best ways of doing this is by comparing qualifications with one another and by really focusing on what it is that you would like to do afterwards. Let's start by comparing the qualifications with one another.

One of the reasons why the Government introduced the 'National Qualifications Framework' (NQF) is so that the various qualifications could be more easily compared. It's worth remembering that only qualifications recognised by the regulatory authorities are included in the NQF. The framework has recently been reviewed and an outline is given below (pay special attention to Level 3):

Qualification level	What it means	Examples of qualifications or awards
Entry level	Involves learning basic knowledge and skills not geared towards specific occupations.	Qualifications are offered at Entry 1, 2, and 3 in a range of subjects

Qualification level	What it means	Examples of qualifications or awards
Level 1	Learning at this level is about activities that relate to everyday situations and possibly job competence.	NVQ 1; certificates in manual skills; GCSEs Grades D–G
Level 2	Learning at this level involves building knowledge and/or skills in relation to an area of work or a subject area and is appropriate for many job roles.	GCSEs Grades A*–C; NVQ 2; some certificates and diplomas; apprenticeships
Level 3	Learning at this level involves obtaining detailed knowledge and skills. It is appropriate for people wishing to go to university, people working independently, or – in some areas – supervising and training others in their field of work.	A levels and AS levels; NVQ 3; Advanced Extension Awards (AEAs); A levels in Applied Subjects; BTEC National Diplomas/Certificates/Awards; Scottish Highers; IB; Welsh Baccalaureate; OCR Nationals
Level 4	Learning at this level is appropriate for people working in technical and professional jobs, and/or managing and developing others. Level 4 qualifications are at a level equivalent to Certificates of Higher Education.	BTEC HND/HNC; NVQ 4; qualifications in some non-graduate professional areas
Level 5	Learning at this level involves the demonstration of high levels of knowledge, a high level of work expertise in job roles and competence in managing and training others. Qualifications at this level are appropriate for people working as higher-grade technicians, professionals or managers.	NVQ 5; Higher Education Diplomas; Foundation degrees
Level 6	Learning at this level involves the achievement of a high level of professional knowledge and is appropriate for people working as knowledge-based professionals or in professional management positions.	Honours Bachelor's degrees; Postgraduate Diplomas in some professional areas (eg Management, Counselling etc)

Qualification level	What it means	Examples of qualifications or awards
Level 7	Learning at this level involves the mastery of a complex and specialised area of knowledge and skills. This level is important for people who want to work in highly specialised or research-based areas.	Master's degrees; some specialist postgraduate diplomas or certificates
Level 8	Achievement at this level involves making a significant and original contribution to a specialised field of enquiry. It is appropriate for people at the forefront of a field of work or research and who want to be pioneers in that area.	Doctorates; specialist awards

In all probability, you will be choosing something from Level 3, but it is useful to see the other levels so you can compare what and how you will be studying. Level 3 qualifications are, in the vast majority of cases, the gateway to higher education and certain jobs.

The UCAS Tariff

Another way of comparing qualifications is to look at the UCAS Tariff for each one. The UCAS Tariff is a points system used to report achievement for entry to higher education (HE) in a numerical format. In other words, institutions usually require a certain number of points to allow you to study there. Many employers also have a points threshold when selecting candidates. This system establishes agreed equivalences between different types of qualification and provides comparisons between applicants with different types and volumes of achievement. Points can be aggregated from the different qualifications included in the Tariff but there is no ceiling to the number of points that can be accumulated. Equally, there is no double counting – applicants cannot count the same or similar qualifications twice. Achievement at a lower level will be subsumed into the higher level, ie AS points will be subsumed into the A level points for the same subject. The same principle applies to Scottish Highers and Advanced Highers, Applied A levels and so on.

The table on the next page shows how the UCAS Tariff works in practice for various different qualifications. (VCEs have been included in the table as these are still being awarded. Points awarded for Applied A level Double awards will be the same as those for VCE Double awards.)

GCE AS/AS VCE	GCE AS Double Award	GCE A level/AVCE	GCE/AVCE Double Award	BTEC Award	BTEC Certificate	BTEC Diploma	OCR Certificate	OCR Diploma	OCR Extended Diploma	Points	Irish Higher	Irish Ordinary	Advanced Higher	Higher	Int 2	Standard Grade
			AA			DDD			D1	360						
			AB			DDM			D2/M1	320						
			BB			DMM			M2	280						
			BC		DD	MMM		D	M3	240						
										220						
			CC		DM	MMP		M1	P1	200						
										180						
			CD		MM	MPP		M2/P1	P2	160						
										140						
	AA	A	DD	D	MP	PPP	D	P2	P3	120			A			
	AB									110						
	BB	B								100			B			
	BC				PP					90	A1					
	CC	C	DE	M			M	P3		80			C			
										77	A2			A		
										72			D			
										71	B1					
	CD									70						
										64	B2			B		
A	DD	D								60						
										58	B3					
										52	C1					
B	DE									50				C		
										48	C2					
							P			45					A	
										42				D		
C	EE	E	EE	P						40						
										39	C3	A1				
										38					B	Band 1
										35						
										33	D1					
D										30						
										28		A2			C	Band 2
										26		B1				
E										20		B2				
										14		B3				
										7						

[1] The points shown are for the newly specified BTEC National Award, Certificate and Diploma introduced into centres from September 2002
[2] The points for the OCR Nationals come into effect for entry to higher education from 2007 onwards. The points for the OCR Nationals come into effect into centres from 2007 onwards.
[3] The points shown for the Irish Leaving Certificate Higher and Ordinary levels come into effect for entry to higher education from 2006 onwards

BTEC Nationals in Early Years[4]			CACHE Diploma in Child Care & Education		Diploma in Foundation Studies (Art and Design)[5]	Points	Music Examinations[6]					
Theory		Practical	Theory	Practical			Practical			Theory		
Certificate	Diploma						Grade 6	Grade 7	Grade 8	Grade 6	Grade 7	Grade 8
	DDD					320						
					Distinction	285						
	DDM		AA			280						
	DMM					240						
					Merit	225						
			BB			220						
DD	MMM					200						
					Pass	165						
DM	MMP		CC			160						
MM	MPP	D	DD	A		120						
				B		100						
MP	PPP	M	EE	C		80						
						75			D			
						70			M			
				D		60		D	P			
						55		M				
						45	D	P				
PP		P		E		40	M					
						30	P					
						25						
						20				D	D	
						15				M	M	D
						10				P	P	M
						5						P

4 The new allocation of points for the theory and practical elements of the BTEC Nationals in Early Years comes into effect for entry to higher education from **2007** onwards
5 Points for the Diploma in Foundation Studies (Art and Design) come into effect for entry to higher education from **2006** onwards
6 Points shown are for ABRSM, Guildhall, LCMM, Rockschool and Trinity Guildhall advanced-level music examinations

Free-standing Maths[7]	IFS CeFS[8]	IFS DipFS[9]	ASDAN COPE[10]	Advanced Extension Awards[11]	Points	Core Skills[12]	Key Skills[13]	Welsh Baccalaureate Core[14]
			Pass		120			Pass
		A			70			
	A	B			60			
	B	C			50			
	C	D		Distinction	40			
	D	E			30		Level 4	
	E			Merit	20	Higher	Level 3	
					17			
					13			
					10	Int 2	Level 2	
					7			

7 Covers free-standing Mathematics qualifications – Additional Maths, Using and Applying Statistics, Working with Algebraic and Graphical Techniques, Modelling with Calculus
8 Points shown are for the revised Institute of Financial Services Certificate in Financial Studies (CeFS) taught from September 2003
9 Points shown are for the Institute of Financial Services Diploma in Financial Studies (DipFS) and come into effect for entry to higher education in 2008
10 Points for ASDAN's Certificate of Personal Effectiveness (COPE) come into effect for entry to higher education in 2007
11 Points for Advanced Extension Awards are over and above those gained from the A level grade and come into effect for entry to higher education in 2006
12 Covers the five Scottish Core Skills – Communication, Information Technology, Numeracy, Problem Solving and Working with Others
13 Covers the main three Key Skills' subjects – Application of Number, Communication and Information Technology, with the three Wider Key Skills (Improving Own Learning and Performance, Problem Solving, Working With Others) coming into effect for 2007 entry
14 Points for the Core are awarded only when a candidate achieves the Welsh Baccalaureate Advanced Diploma

If you are still having difficulty deciding which is the most appropriate post-16 qualification for you, the following exercise should help you. Look at the statement on the left-hand side and see if it applies to you. If it does, then look at the corresponding qualification(s) on the right-hand side of the table.

Does this statement apply to you?	Most appropriate qualification(s)
I want a qualification that will give me a practical skill towards a specific job.	Apprenticeships; NVQs 1 and 2
I want an academic qualification that will help me get into university in the UK, but not necessarily related to any particular occupation.	A levels and AS levels; International Baccalaureate; Welsh Baccalaureate; Scottish Highers; BTEC Nationals
I want to go to university in Europe.	International Baccalaureate
I want to study something of a high academic standard, which would allow me to go to university, but related to a particular sector of work.	Applied A levels
I want a practical, skills-based qualification that will show that I can do a certain job at a high level.	NVQ 3 and 4
I excel in a particular subject and I would like to study it at a higher level before I go to university.	Advanced Extension Awards (AEAs)
I want to get a recognised qualification in child care education that would also give me some points towards university entry.	CACHE Diploma
I want to build on my practical skills in art and design and study it at a higher-education level.	Diploma in Foundation Studies (Art and Design)

The next section focuses on choosing between specific subjects, mainly with A levels in mind. If you need more specific subject information on other Level 3 qualifications, look at the relevant websites listed on page 15.

Choosing your subjects

This section includes:
- » **answers to the most common questions asked by prospective students**
- » **exercises to help you decide between subjects**
- » **a breakdown of the A level results from summer 2004**
- » **sources of further information.**

This section will look at the kinds of things to consider when you're trying to choose between different subjects: this is one of the dilemmas that students face when thinking about their options. The following questions tend to be the most frequently asked.

Should I choose those subjects I am strongest in?

This is as good a reason as any to choose a subject at Advanced level. Think about the subjects you've studied so far at GCSE and which ones you've had the best results in. This should give you the confidence that you could study it at a higher level. There is quite a jump in difficulty between GCSE and Level 3 qualifications.

Should I choose those subjects I enjoy the most?

It's possible to be good at a subject and not enjoy it – and vice versa. However, experience shows that those who go for subjects they are really interested in tend to do better. This is largely because they have a natural talent for that area but also because they are likely to have the motivation to do the reading around the subject that is needed to get the top grades. One word of warning, though: if you go for subjects that you enjoy, check which HE courses you are ruling out by making this choice.

If you are struggling to think about what your natural talents are, the following table might help you. Look at the skills on the left-hand side of the table and decide which ones you'd definitely like to use in further study, and those you definitely wouldn't like to use. Put a tick or a cross in each case. Then look to see which subjects match which skills, and see if that sheds any light on where your natural talents lie.

Name of skill	I like using this skill	I hate using this skill	Subjects that require this skill a lot
Communication skills (good at communicating, reading, writing essays, learning languages)			All subjects, but especially arts, humanities and social science subjects such as English, History, Sociology, modern languages, Media and Communication
Attention to detail (being good with small details, checking facts, figures, specifics, quantities)			All science subjects, as well as Geography, History, Engineering, Archaeology, ICT, Geology
Physical ability (eg making things, doing things, exercising, using your hands, doing experiments)			Physical Education, science subjects, Engineering, Archaeology, ICT, Photography, Art and Design, Design and Technology
Creative ability (eg making things, writing or drawing, performing)			Art and Design, Design and Technology, English Literature, Drama, Performing Arts, Music
Memory and recall skills (memorising facts, words, vocabulary and theories)			Many subjects, but especially History, Mathematics, science subjects, Philosophy, modern languages, Latin/Greek

Name of skill	I like using this skill	I hate using this skill	Subjects that require this skill a lot
ICT and computing skills (using hardware, software and systems)			ICT/Computing, Archaeology, Design and Technology, Music Technology, Engineering, Physics, Technology, Geology
Mathematical skills (using figures and stats to conclude and investigate things; doing mental calculations).			Mathematics, all sciences (especially Physics), Engineering, Psychology, Design and Technology, Geography, Geology
Emotional intelligence skills (empathising, intuition, vision, creativity, tact, interpersonal skills)			Religious Studies, English Literature, History of Art, Communication Studies, Psychology, History, Classical Civilisation, Music
Spatial awareness and mechanical skills (being able to 'see' what shapes will fit where; making and working with mechanical objects)			Engineering, Physics, Art and Design, Design and Technology, Computing/ICT, Construction and the Built Environment
Business skills (understanding business, finance and economics, as well as specific sectors of work)			Accounting, Business Studies, Economics, Law, Travel and Tourism, Retail and Distributive Services, Leisure and Recreation
Citizenship skills (being familiar with and learning about social, political and environmental issues of the past and present)			Ancient History, Classical Civilisation, Geography, History, Environmental Science, Politics and Government, Law, Philosophy, Latin/Greek, Sociology, Social Policy, Religious Studies, English Literature, Media Studies

How are the different subjects assessed?

Most A levels, AS Levels and equivalents such as Scottish Highers are assessed by a combination of written exams (either during or at the end of your course), coursework (essays, projects or case studies) completed during the course in your own time, and practical exams (especially for science subjects or others for which certain practical skills are needed). Not only are there variations between subjects in terms of the type of assessment, but there also will be some variation between different examination boards offering the same subject. So try to work out whether you are better at exams, coursework or practical work and bear that in mind when choosing your particular subjects.

Which subjects are best to get into higher education?

That very much depends on what you want to study. If you already know you want to study a particular subject at university, then in most cases it's expected that you have an A level or equivalent with a good grade in that subject. However, there are some subjects where it's not clear which subject areas are required because that subject isn't widely offered (if at all) at Level 3. Also, some degree subjects specify more than one particular A level or equivalent. The table below explains, using some of the most popular subjects as examples.

Most other degree subjects not mentioned on this list require an A level in that subject at the specified grade plus required grades in other subjects.

Type of degree	Subjects usually required at A level (or equivalent)
Law	Any subjects
Engineering	Mathematics and Physics
Medicine	Chemistry and one or two other sciences
Physics	Physics and Mathematics
Dentistry	Chemistry (and sometimes Biology)
Veterinary Science	Chemistry (and sometimes Biology)
Modern languages	Usually you need to have studied the language at A level

Type of degree	Subjects usually required at A level (or equivalent)
Sociology	Any subjects at the required grade. At least one humanities subject could be useful
Politics	Any subjects at the required grade. At least one humanities subject could be useful
Philosophy	Any subjects at the required grade. At least one humanities subject could be useful

Should I choose subjects that are similar to one another?

That partly depends on the kind of person you are. Some people like to specialise (and, for example, take all science or all arts subjects); others prefer to have a taste of both. It doesn't really matter as long as you know the UCAS requirements for your higher-education course or the grades needed for the kind of job you're interested in. However, do make sure that there is not too much overlap between subjects, as this might detrimentally affect your UCAS points total.

How can I choose between similar subjects?

A common issue for many is choosing between similar subjects, eg between French and German or between English Language and English Literature. The following outline should give you an idea of some of the differences between apparently similar subjects.

Subjects	Similarities and differences
English Language vs English Literature	There are some crossovers in that both subjects involve a lot of reading and essay writing. The main difference is that in Literature the focus will be on analysing novels, poems and plays and looking at the themes from many different angles. In Language, you will be looking at such things as the structure of the English language (syntax, grammar, verbs and so on) as well as how the language has developed over time. If you like both, then you could consider doing an A level in English Language and Literature – some (but not all) schools offer this option.

Subjects	Similarities and differences
Economics vs Business Studies	Economics studies the broad trends of economic activity, including markets, house prices, exchange rates, inflation and so on. In Business Studies, the focus is more on the different elements needed for a successful business.
The sciences	Choosing which science(s) to study can be difficult, since they all involve elements of analysis, practical work and experimentation. Biology has the most emphasis on living things on earth, including humans; Chemistry's focus is more on the chemical processes that take place around us and how those processes can be applied to different contexts; Physics looks at the laws of nature such as gravity, forces, electricity, the nature of the atom, and so on. Physics and Chemistry in general require a higher level of numerical ability than Biology. Entry to some degree programmes depends on your studying a particular science, so check before you choose!
Sociology vs Social Policy	These subjects examine similar themes. However, Sociology focuses on how people behave in groups and how they are influenced by them; Social Policy is more about identifying existing (government) policies on social issues (eg homelessness) and perhaps also identifying further areas where social policy is needed.
History vs Geography	The age-old rivalry! Although these subjects call on similar skills, they are very different in content. Geography is about our environment (weather, ecosystems, natural hazards, etc) as well as how humans fit into it. History is about interpreting the past using different sources. There is probably a larger amount of reading and writing in History, but you may have to analyse many more different types of data in Geography.

Subjects	Similarities and differences
Media Studies vs Communication Studies	Communication Studies is about analysing all types of different communication, from body language to the internet. Media Studies is more specifically about the media and media products such as radio, TV, film, advertising and so on.
Modern languages	Choosing between different foreign languages can be tricky. In the eyes of an employer it doesn't really matter unless you have a very specific career in mind. What will count most is which one you enjoy, which one you will find most useful and which teacher you get on with best! English, Spanish and French are the most international languages so in that sense are the most useful.
Music vs Music Technology	Music Technology is about how technology has influenced music; Music is much more about developing your musical skills and knowledge – you will need to study 'pure' Music if you want to study it at degree level.
Archaeology vs Ancient History	These are very different subjects. Archaeologists learn about how to get evidence of past civilisations from physical remains and other data sources. Ancient History focuses specifically on the civilisation and culture of Ancient Rome and Greece.
GCE A level Drama and Theatre Studies vs Performing Arts	Performing Arts does cover theatre and drama, but it also covers areas such as dance, singing, music and arts administration. A level Drama and Performance focuses solely on that medium. The course in Performing Arts tends to have a more vocational focus too.
Applied Art and Design vs Design and Technology	There are some overlaps but Art and Design focuses more on areas such as fine art, 3-D design, textiles, graphic design and photography, whereas Design and Technology is more about the properties of materials (eg wood, metal, plastic) and how they can be manipulated to produce something. There is also more of a vocational emphasis in the first subject.

Do I need a GCSE in a subject to do it at GCE A level?

Not necessarily. If you can convince your tutors or teachers that you have the right academic potential as well as the right attitude, then it is possible – in some cases. However, there are subjects that really build on the knowledge you've learned at GCSE. These include:

» Mathematics
» Sciences
» Languages.

It would be difficult to pick these subjects up at A level without any of the building blocks. There are, however, subjects that are not studied at GCSE level, which most people meet for the first time at A level and which assume no prior knowledge. These include, among others:

» Law
» Sociology
» Business
» Philosophy
» Government and Politics.

Which A levels are easiest to get good grades in?

This depends on what you are best at and what you enjoy – chances are, that's how you will get the best grades. However, every year figures are produced on the GCE A level results by the Joint Council for General Qualifications. The results for summer 2004 are given below. Be careful, though: do not use the table as an indication of the level of difficulty of a subject and base your choice on that, as there will be many contributing factors as to why one subject gains more top grades than another.

Subject	Gender	Number sat	% of total no. sat	Percentages by grade					
				A	B	C	D	E	U
Art and design subjects[1]	Male	12,428	3.5	22.8	21.9	22.9	17.7	10.1	4.6
	Female	26,561	6.4	30.3	25.2	21.8	14.0	6.3	2.4
	All	38,989	5.1	27.9	24.2	22.1	15.2	7.5	3.1
Biology	Male	20,761	5.9	20.3	20.5	20.1	17.7	13.9	7.5
	Female	31,503	7.6	23.8	21.8	20.6	16.5	11.3	6.0
	All	52,264	6.8	22.4	21.3	20.4	17.0	12.3	6.6

Subject	Gender	Number sat	% of total no. sat	Percentages by grade					
				A	B	C	D	E	U
Business Studies	Male	18,930	5.4	13.0	23.5	28.0	22.0	10.3	3.2
	Female	13,323	3.2	15.7	25.1	27.0	20.4	9.3	2.5
	All	32,253	4.2	14.1	24.2	27.5	21.4	9.9	2.9
Chemistry	Male	18,311	5.2	29.2	22.9	19.0	14.2	9.9	4.8
	Female	18,943	4.6	30.6	25.3	18.9	13.4	8.2	3.6
	All	37,254	4.9	29.9	24.1	19.0	13.8	9.0	4.2
Classical subjects'	Male	2454	0.7	33.0	25.1	22.8	12.5	4.8	1.8
	Female	3335	0.8	35.0	29.4	20.1	11.3	3.2	1.0
	All	5789	0.8	34.1	27.7	21.2	11.8	3.9	1.3
Communication Studies	Male	743	0.2	15.6	21.3	26.0	22.4	11.2	3.5
	Female	1567	0.4	21.6	25.6	28.5	16.8	6.3	1.2
	All	2310	0.3	19.7	24.2	27.7	18.6	7.9	1.9
Computing	Male	7456	2.1	13.4	19.3	22.3	21.8	15.6	7.6
	Female	1032	0.2	17.4	20.5	21.9	21.0	12.7	6.5
	All	8488	1.1	13.9	19.4	22.3	21.7	15.3	7.4
Economics	Male	12,067	3.4	28.9	26.2	21.9	14.0	6.6	2.4
	Female	5695	1.4	33.0	27.5	20.7	12.1	5.0	1.7
	All	17,762	2.3	30.2	26.6	21.6	13.4	6.0	2.2
English'	Male	24,728	7.0	20.9	23.0	26.0	20.1	8.1	1.9
	Female	56,921	13.8	20.4	24.1	27.5	19.5	7.1	1.4
	All	81,649	10.7	20.6	23.7	27.1	19.6	7.4	1.6
Expressive Arts/Drama	Male	4786	1.4	12.2	25.4	31.5	20.7	8.2	2.0
	Female	13,045	3.2	15.9	29.7	32.4	16.2	4.8	1.0
	All	17,831	2.3	14.9	28.5	32.2	17.4	5.8	1.2
French	Male	4914	1.4	34.7	26.4	19.2	11.7	6.2	1.8
	Female	10,235	2.5	32.8	26.9	20.1	13.0	5.7	1.5
	All	15,149	2.0	33.4	26.8	19.8	12.6	5.8	1.6
General Studies	Male	27,776	7.9	11.2	16.5	21.5	23.2	17.1	10.5
	Female	30,540	7.4	12.4	17.8	23.3	22.8	15.7	8.0
	All	58,316	7.6	11.8	17.2	22.4	23.1	16.3	9.2
Geography	Male	18,762	5.3	19.9	25.6	25.3	18.3	8.7	2.2
	Female	15,453	3.7	29.0	28.6	22.4	13.2	5.5	1.3
	All	34,215	4.5	24.0	27.0	24.0	16.0	7.2	1.8

Subject	Gender	Number sat	% of total no. sat	Percentages by grade					
				A	B	C	D	E	U
German	Male	2269	0.6	35.3	23.6	17.4	14.2	6.9	2.6
	Female	4121	1.0	31.4	25.0	20.5	14.6	6.8	1.7
	All	6390	0.8	32.8	24.5	19.4	14.4	6.9	2.0
History	Male	21,794	6.2	22.4	25.1	25.2	16.9	8.0	2.4
	Female	21,996	5.3	25.5	27.6	23.6	15.1	6.4	1.8
	All	43,790	5.7	23.9	26.5	24.3	16.0	7.2	2.1
Home Economics	Male	60	0.0	5.0	11.7	25.0	20.0	26.6	11.7
	Female	1112	0.3	17.8	28.1	25.4	18.8	7.5	2.4
	All	1172	0.2	17.2	27.2	25.4	18.9	8.4	2.9
Information and Communication Technology	Male	10,479	3.0	6.4	15.2	24.2	27.4	18.7	8.1
	Female	5627	1.4	8.8	19.8	27.3	24.6	14.3	5.2
	All	16,106	2.1	7.3	16.7	25.4	26.3	17.3	7.0
Irish	Male	122	0.0	42.6	26.3	16.3	9.9	1.6	3.3
	Female	164	0.0	43.9	30.5	16.5	6.1	2.4	0.6
	All	286	0.0	43.4	28.6	16.5	7.7	2.1	1.7
Law	Male	5558	1.6	14.1	19.9	22.8	20.8	14.1	8.3
	Female	8371	2.0	19.3	21.7	23.3	18.2	10.9	6.6
	All	13,929	1.8	17.2	21.0	23.1	19.2	12.2	7.3
Mathematics	Male	32,379	9.2	36.5	20.5	16.6	12.5	8.5	5.4
	Female	20,409	4.9	40.1	22.6	16.4	10.6	6.6	3.7
	All	52,788	6.9	37.9	21.3	16.5	11.7	7.8	4.8
Mathematics (Further)	Male	4096	1.2	58.2	17.0	10.8	7.1	4.6	2.3
	Female	1624	0.4	60.5	16.7	10.5	6.4	4.2	1.7
	All	5720	0.7	58.9	16.8	10.8	6.9	4.4	2.2
Media/Film/TV Studies[1]	Male	12,141	3.4	11.0	24.4	32.6	22.4	7.3	2.3
	Female	14,753	3.6	15.9	30.4	30.9	16.8	4.7	1.3
	All	26,894	3.5	13.7	27.7	31.6	19.3	5.9	1.8
Modern languages[2] (all)	Male	2538	0.7	38.0	31.5	16.6	6.9	3.7	3.3
	Female	3485	0.8	45.9	29.5	13.2	6.3	2.7	2.4
	All	6023	0.8	42.6	30.3	14.6	6.6	3.2	2.7
Music	Male	4644	1.3	17.8	21.8	23.6	20.6	11.0	5.2
	Female	4636	1.1	24.2	24.9	23.6	16.7	8.4	2.2
	All	9280	1.2	21.0	23.3	23.6	18.7	9.7	3.7

Subject	Gender	Number sat	% of total no. sat	Percentages by grade					
				A	B	C	D	E	U
Physics	Male	22,293	6.3	27.0	19.8	19.0	15.9	11.6	6.7
	Female	6405	1.5	33.4	23.5	18.0	13.3	8.3	3.5
	All	28,698	3.7	28.4	20.7	18.8	15.2	10.9	6.0
Political Studies	Male	6074	1.7	24.9	28.9	22.2	14.5	6.4	3.1
	Female	4139	1.0	30.5	28.4	20.6	12.6	5.5	2.4
	All	10,213	1.3	27.2	28.7	21.5	13.8	6.0	2.8
Psychology	Male	11,875	3.4	11.0	18.9	24.0	22.2	16.2	7.7
	Female	35,058	8.5	20.1	24.0	23.7	17.9	9.9	4.4
	All	46,933	6.1	17.8	22.7	23.8	18.9	11.5	5.3
Religious Studies	Male	4137	1.2	24.6	28.9	24.5	13.8	5.9	2.3
	Female	10,281	2.5	25.1	31.0	23.9	13.6	5.0	1.4
	All	14,418	1.9	24.9	30.5	24.1	13.6	5.2	1.7
Science subjects[2]	Male	3220	0.9	22.1	19.0	22.1	18.1	13.5	5.2
	Female	1224	0.3	19.3	21.4	23.2	20.5	11.2	4.4
	All	4444	0.6	21.4	19.6	22.4	18.8	12.8	5.0
Sociology	Male	6138	1.7	13.8	23.2	26.3	21.5	10.4	4.8
	Female	19,433	4.7	19.7	25.4	26.0	18.0	7.9	3.0
	All	25,571	3.3	18.3	24.9	26.0	18.9	8.5	3.4
Spanish	Male	1852	0.5	37.6	28.0	18.7	9.2	4.3	2.2
	Female	4114	1.0	34.1	27.7	20.5	11.2	4.8	1.7
	All	5966	0.8	35.2	27.7	20.0	10.6	4.6	1.9
Sport/PE Studies	Male	12,324	3.5	8.0	17.6	25.6	26.6	16.8	5.4
	Female	7265	1.8	18.5	23.6	24.4	19.6	10.4	3.5
	All	19,589	2.6	11.9	19.8	25.2	24.0	14.4	4.7
Technology subjects[1]	Male	10,752	3.0	12.7	20.6	25.8	22.8	13.6	4.5
	Female	6509	1.6	19.8	24.9	25.9	18.1	9.2	2.1
	All	17,261	2.3	15.4	22.2	25.9	21.0	11.9	3.6
Welsh[4]	Male	181	0.1	19.9	20.4	29.3	23.8	3.8	2.8
	Female	738	0.2	21.4	24.8	32.3	14.0	6.0	1.5
	All	919	0.1	21.1	23.9	31.7	16.0	5.6	1.7
All other subjects	Male	3593	1.0	13.0	17.6	22.3	21.8	15.5	9.8
	Female	3995	1.0	19.3	21.9	22.2	18.0	11.9	6.7
	All	7588	1.0	16.3	19.9	22.2	19.8	13.6	8.2

Subject	Gender	Number sat	% of total no. sat	Percentages by grade					
				A	B	C	D	E	U
All subjects	Male	352,635	100.0	21.0	21.7	22.8	18.6	10.9	5.0
	Female	413,612	100.0	23.7	24.6	23.6	16.6	8.3	3.2
	All	766,247	100.0	22.4	23.4	23.2	17.5	9.5	4.0

[1] Covers a range of related subjects
[2] Includes all science subjects except Biology, Chemistry and Physics
[3] Includes all languages except Irish, French, German, Spanish and Welsh
[4] Includes Welsh (First Language) and Welsh (Second Language)

(Published by the Joint Council for Qualifications, 19 August 2004)

For information about AEA and AS level results from last year, visit www.jcq.org.uk.

How can I find out more?
If you need further information at this point, it's worth remembering the following sources of information can be very useful.

» Tutors
» UCAS – the central admissions organisation for entry into higher education (visit www.ucas.com)
» The admissions departments of universities you're interested in applying to
» Trotman Publishing website: www.trotman.co.uk
» Connexions Services, who give advice and guidance for young people. Visit www.connexions.gov.uk.

By now you should have lots of information about what to consider when choosing your subjects. Once you've come up with a shortlist, go to Part Two to look at the relevant subject areas in detail. This should confirm your choices, or it may make you reconsider. Either way, it's essential information before you make your final decision.

PART TWO:
A TO Z OF A LEVELS
AND AS LEVELS

How to use the directory

The following directory of subjects is based on GCE A levels and AS levels. It does not include every single subject that it's possible to study, but it does outline the vast majority on offer. Some of the information could apply to alternative qualifications, but you should always refer to the specific syllabus you are studying.

Each subject is covered under the following sections:

- » Overview of the area
- » Main elements of the course
- » How is it taught and assessed?
- » Choosing other A level subjects to go with it
- » The subject at higher-education level
- » A degree in the subject
- » Combining it with other subjects at degree level
- » Foundation degrees and HNDs
- » The subject and your future career.

Syllabus information
If you need more information on any subject that interests you, it's a good idea to check out the syllabus of the relevant exam board that your school or college runs. These can be found on the exam-board websites listed below.

Foundation degrees and HNDs
The availability of these courses is listed separately in each subject section. Foundation degrees are offered in the whole range of subjects but are usually vocationally based and include work experience. They last two years and can be converted to a full degree.

Higher National Diplomas (HNDs) are similar to Foundation degrees in that they tend to be vocationally based and can be converted to diplomas or full degrees.

Future careers

Each subject area contains ideas for possible future careers for both non-graduates and graduates. It is estimated that about 60% of graduate jobs are open to students irrespective of their degree subject. What tends to interest employers most is previous experience, skills, potential and personal qualities. It's important to get involved in outside activities while you're a student so that a whole range of employers will be interested in your portfolio of skills and abilities.

What to do next

As you browse the directory, try to have in mind the following questions:

» Would I enjoy studying this?
» Would I do well in the subject, given the type of assessment methods used?
» How would choosing this subject affect my higher-education options?
» How would choosing this subject affect my career options?

Then come up with a shortlist of subjects. If you are still finding it difficult to choose between a few subjects, look back at 'Choosing your subjects' in Part One, page 24.

Useful contacts and sources of further information

Qualifications and Curriculum Authority
QCA Customer Relations
83 Piccadilly
London W1J 8QA
Tel (enquiries): 020 7509 5556
Website: www.qca.org.uk

Exam boards
AQA
Stag Hill House
Guildford
Surrey GU2 7XJ
Tel: 01483 506506
Website: www.aqa.org.uk

CCEA
29 Clarendon Road
Clarendon Dock
Belfast BT1 3BG
Tel: 028 9026 1200
Website: www.ccea.org.uk

Edexcel
190 High Holborn
London WC1V 7BH
Tel: 0870 240 9800
Website: www.edexcel.org.uk

OCR
9 Hills Road
Cambridge CB2 1PB
Tel: 01223 553311
Website: www.ocr.org.uk

WJEC
245 Western Avenue
Cardiff CF5 2YX
Tel: 029 2026 5000
Website: www.wjec.co.uk

Accounting

Good financial information is a key requirement for success in most areas of life. It is essential for businesses, for governments, for households and for individuals. Traditionally, accountants had to do two things: provide a record of trading activity and act as independent auditors of the activity. Accountants learn this, but they also deal with issues such as tax liabilities, act as company directors or work with senior managers in business to help them plan their commercial activities.

Accounting is divided into two main areas: financial accounting and management accounting. The former deals with checking a company's accounts and preparing the annual accounts; management accountants usually work for a particular company and assist managers with budgeting and financial planning.

Students of A level Accounting will learn much of this and therefore they will need a keen interest in business, good attention to detail and a sound head for figures. If you struggled with GCSE Mathematics, this may not be the subject for you.

Main elements of the course

The outline below is based on what the majority of A level exam-board syllabuses include. For an exact definition of the AS and A2 syllabus you will be studying, you should consult your school or college or even the exam board itself.

Financial accounting

This is a major part of the course and will include some, if not all, of the following:

» Understanding how accountancy works – the Accounting Information System
» Introduction to published accounts of limited companies
» Determination of income – ie what you have to take into account to determine the true income of an organisation
» Accounting standards – understanding the national and international standards of accounting practice.

Management accounting

» Budgeting and budgetary analysis – understanding spending patterns and predicting future needs
» Types of costing – understanding indirect costs, such as overheads, that aren't directly a part of making an organisation profitable
» Break-even analysis – working out how much a business needs to make before it covers its costs and how much it needs to sell before making a profit
» Capital investment appraisal – evaluating the pros and cons of investing money.

Each of these elements has further sub-sections, so students should check with the school or exam board for the exact details.

How is Accounting taught and assessed?
In the first instance, students will be introduced to the principles of accounting and then, over time, they will start to apply the principles to real situations. Therefore, the experience of studying this subject will be a mixture of learning theories and applying principles to business case studies.

A lot of database and spreadsheet work is needed for this subject, as are many mathematical calculations. Even though GCSE Accounting is not required for studying the subject at A level, an aptitude for mathematics is very useful. Students are also trained how to write business reports that include financial recommendations. In most cases, students have to write a series of these for their A2 or AS examinations. Coursework assessment is usually at a minimum in this A level and the ability to write analytical reports under pressure will determine a student's success.

Choosing other A level subjects to go with Accounting
Popular choices include Business Studies, Computing, Law, Economics, Mathematics and some science subjects. If you want to study Accounting at degree level, be aware that some universities require A level Mathematics. For other degree subjects (mainly arts and humanities) at

some universities A level Accounting is not recognised as an entry qualification. If you already know what and where you want to study at a higher level, always check with the institution before finally choosing your subject.

Accounting at higher-education level

Given that Accounting is still not as established an A level as some other subjects, most universities do not require A level Accounting as an entry prerequisite for their degree course. In fact, some prefer more 'traditional' A levels than Accounting or Business Studies. Most usually require a good grade at A level Mathematics, however. Many degree courses are called Accounting and Finance rather than just Accounting and some include elements of Economics and Computing.

A degree in Accounting?

At degree level, Accounting usually covers some core modules in both the first and second years and there are usually some further options that students can choose in their final year. One thing to consider when choosing your higher-education course is whether or not it gives you the opportunity to gain exemption from professional accountancy examinations. Some courses do, some don't.

Combining Accounting with other subjects

Accounting can be combined with almost any other subject, but popular ones include: Economics, Computing, Business Management, Law, Finance, Mathematics and many others. However, as mentioned above, be careful when you combine with other subjects: it may affect your exemptions from professional examinations later on.

Foundation degrees and HNDs

A small number of Foundation degrees and HNDs are available in Accounting, and some are also available in various areas of Business, of which accounting would be a part.

Accounting and your future career

Non-graduate jobs

It is possible to become a qualified accountant without going to university. You would have to complete a four-year training contract with a firm of accountants and take the necessary professional studies and examinations. You will need good grades at A level (at least three Cs) and the aptitude and temperament to successfully complete substantial further study. You could also consider working for the accounts department of any organisation as an accounts assistant or an accounts technician.

You would, of course, be able to go for any other jobs that are open to non-graduates. Those that require numerical skills, attention to detail and an interest in business would be suitable for those who have done A level Accounting.

Graduate jobs directly related to Accounting (and Finance)

To obtain a professional accountancy qualification, you will need to follow your degree with further study leading to professional examinations, together with a period of approved work experience.

Various types of accountancy

You could be employed by a firm of accountants providing financial or business advice and other management services to a wide range of fee-paying clients from the private individual to large commercial organisations and government bodies. Or you could be employed by a blue-chip organisation or a public-sector organisation and work with departmental managers to help them understand financial information. There are also many other different accountancy roles open to you.

Graduate jobs in which Accounting (and Finance) would be useful

The knowledge and skills gained in this degree subject would be relevant to jobs across the financial and business sector. Some examples of these areas are:

» **Corporate, commercial and investment banking**: there is a wide range of generalist and specialist jobs in this area. Corporate financiers' tasks include advising clients on raising capital, whereas operations professionals ensure that transactions run smoothly.
» **Financial management**: important in all sectors of business, industry and commerce. There are opportunities to work in the public sector, eg NHS financial management. Large companies may employ corporate treasurers.
» **Insurance and pensions and actuarial work**: jobs in insurance include managing pension funds and underwriting insurance claims.
» **Investment management**: traders and stockbrokers are employed by banks. Not a career choice for the shy and timid!
» **Management consultancy**: management consultants are called in to help solve organisational problems that a company might have. This could be in almost any area including finances, ICT, human resources and so on. It is a competitive area to get into.
» **Retail banking and personal financial services**: bank managers may manage several branches with responsibility for meeting sales targets

and attracting new business. Credit analysts undertake risk assessments on loan requests.

◫ **Taxation**: either as a tax advisor, providing advisory and consultancy services in order to create the best tax strategies for your clients, or as a tax inspector, determining tax liability on behalf of the Inland Revenue.

Further information

Association of Chartered Certified Accountants (ACCA) – www.acca.co.uk
Chartered Institute for Public Finance and Accountancy (CIPFA) – www.cipfa.org.uk
Institute of Chartered Accountants in England and Wales (ICAEW) – www.icaew.co.uk
Chartered Institute of Management Accountants – www.cimaglobal.com
AccountingWeb – www.accountingweb.co.uk

Ancient History

Ancient History is all about the study of two specific parts of the world from which much of our cultural, literary and artistic heritage derives: Greece and Rome. Students look at the origins of these two classical civilisations (dating from between 2000 and 6000 years ago) as well as the empires that developed from them. Students will gain an appreciation of a variety of aspects of Greek and Roman society. This includes cultural aspects such as architecture, literature, sculpture; intellectual aspects such as philosophy and education; spiritual aspects such as religion and morality; and other social factors such as economics, slavery and the role of women.

Students who have GCSE History may be more comfortable with this subject but it is not usually a prerequisite to study this A level.

Main elements of the course
You should check with your school, college or exam board about the precise nature of the course, although at the time of writing, OCR is the only exam board to offer this subject at A level.

Document studies
The ability to appreciate and critically evaluate historical documents is obviously a key skill in this subject. Students are usually asked to examine documents from a particular period of ancient history that they are studying and are asked questions about it. Throughout the course students become practised in this skill, and document study usually forms part of a student's final assessment.

Periods of ancient history

Students study aspects of both Greek and Roman history and will usually include some or all of the following:

» Herodotus and the conflict of Greece and Persia 499–497 BC
» Greek history 446–413 BC
» The culture of Athens 447–399 BC
» Roman history 81–44 BC
» The age of Augustus or Roman history AD 14–68
» Roman Britain AD 43–160.

Study of themes in Greek and Roman history

As with other subjects, Ancient History is also studied by theme as well as by specific periods of time. Some or all of the following themes are usually included:

» The culture of tyranny in the Greek world 600–479 BC
» Sparta in the Greek world 500–420 BC
» Athenian democracy 508–399 BC
» The growth and government of the Roman Empire 133–30 BC
» The City of Rome 33 BC–AD 117
» Emperors and empire AD 14–117
» The Romanisation of Britain AD 43–415.

How is Ancient History taught and assessed?

Teaching is done through class work, lectures and discussions. Students may also look at a variety of influences of ancient culture on today's society such as literature, architecture, philosophy, medicine and much more. Coursework is an option for assessment in this subject, but this depends on whether your school or college chooses this route. Some prefer exams only.

Choosing other A level subjects to go with Ancient History

Other subjects that go well with Ancient History are History, English Literature, Art, languages, Classical Civilisation, Latin and Classical Greek. But, as with all subjects, there is no reason why students can't combine it with science-related or mathematically based subjects.

Ancient History at higher-education level

Ancient History remains a 'niche' subject at university level. However, employers appreciate the skills that historians develop and it is still seen as an academically rigorous discipline. Related courses include Modern

History, Economic History, International History, Political History and many others. In general, you would probably need A level History, Ancient History or Classics to get on to these courses, but this is not always necessary.

A degree in Ancient History?

Like A level Ancient History, the focus of most degree courses will be on ancient Roman and Greek history and civilisation. However, your studies will be much more wide ranging and the subject looked at in much more depth. There may also be a requirement for students to become familiar with written Greek and Latin so that they can analyse historical documents in the original language.

Combining Ancient History with other degree subjects

At university level, Ancient History is often taught by the Classics department rather than the History department. It is sometimes combined with other disciplines to form a joint degree. Such courses include: Ancient History and Classics, Ancient History and Archaeology, Ancient History and Greek and so on.

Foundation degrees and HNDs

Given that Ancient History doesn't have a vocational focus, there is currently no Ancient History Foundation degree. Similarly, there is currently no Diploma available in Ancient History.

Ancient History and your future career

Non-graduate jobs

Many employers requiring A levels do not really mind which subjects applicants have. In that sense, Ancient History A level is as good a choice as any. In fact, there may be some non-graduate areas of work where this A level is still more useful than some others because of the particular skills gained and knowledge acquired. These include:

- Administrative work (such as areas of the Civil Service)
- Management
- Sales
- Marketing
- Working as an assistant in a museum or gallery.

Graduate jobs directly related to Ancient History

The vast majority of careers for which a first degree in a history-related subject is essential or directly relevant require some form of further study or training. Occupations you may wish to consider include the following:

» **Academic librarian/information manager/records manager**: responsible for the acquisition, organisation and dissemination of information and materials within the library system or information unit.
» **Archaeologist**: studies human past through material remains.
» **Archivist**: acquires, selects, arranges, stores, preserves and retrieves records not in current use but deemed to be of historical value.
» **Genealogist**: traces and charts lines of descent or family trees. Possibility of freelance work.
» **Museum/art-gallery curator**: responsible for the care and improvement of a collection including exhibitions, catalogues and acquisitions.
» **Secondary-school teacher**: involved in teaching history to 11–18 year-olds in schools.

Graduate jobs in which Ancient History could be useful

» **Arts administrator**: brings together artists and audiences to support and generate artistic activity.
» **Civil Service fast streamer**: through fast-stream entry, graduates are involved in helping senior staff, as well as formulating and implementing policy. Graduates also enter as junior managers with administrative and management responsibilities.
» **Journalist**: gathers and presents news and features to the public.
» **Local-government administrator**: covers a wide variety of tasks and duties, including co-ordinating and servicing committees, writing reports, drafting policies and procedures, and managing local elections. The work can include liaison within departments as well as with the general public and councillors.
» **Marketing executive, consumer products**: manages the marketing of a product or service from research and development through to the launch. This can include promotion and advertising to the public or businesses.
» **Primary-school teacher**: develops and fosters the appropriate skills and social abilities to enable the optimum development of children, within the framework of the National Curriculum.
» **Solicitor**: advises individuals and organisations on legal aspects of personal and business problems.

Further information
Council for British Archaeology – www.britarch.ac.uk
Historical Association – www.history.org.uk
Museums Association – www.museumsassociation.org

Archaeology

Archaeology literally means the study of ancient things. In particular, it's about understanding history by studying relics and antiquities that have been excavated from the land beneath our feet. This subject draws on other disciplines such as information technology, science and literature, but its closest ally is History. In the absence of any written records, archaeology is often the only other means of identifying key events and civilisations of the past. Students of A level Archaeology learn, among other things, how sites are identified for excavation, how to interpret and date the findings, and how settlements are formed.

Main elements of the course

The outline below is based on what the majority of A level exam-board syllabuses include. For an exact definition of the AS and A2 syllabus you will be studying, you should consult your school or college or even the exam board itself. Students for the AS award will study 50% of the modules that are needed for the A2 award.

Survey and excavation

In this module students learn about how and why sites are excavated, how to carry out fieldwork, using aerial photographs, understanding the environment and working with the community, detecting objects in the earth (using techniques such as metal detection) and techniques for carrying out surveys.

Post-excavation, dating and interpretation (techniques and methods)

In this aspect of the course, students learn how to analyse the material they have recorded from a survey or excavation, typology, environmental analysis including pollen dating, general principles of chemical and physical analysis, and how to date and interpret recorded material using a variety of techniques.

Religion and ritual
This module is about archaeological information and what it tells us about religion and ritual from various cultures. Schools can choose to apply this in a variety of contexts, including prehistoric Britain and Ireland, Ancient Egypt, the Mayan age and the Roman world to AD 476.

Settlement and social organisation
This aspect of the course introduces students to the various different types of settlement that archaeologists study and excavate, including domestic, agricultural, public or religious settlements. Social organisation teaches students how they can realistically assume what a particular society was like using the archaeological evidence.

Material culture and technology
This module of the course introduces the study of art and artefacts, how societies in the past grew food and exploited animal and vegetable resources for survival and for trade, and how they transported those resources.

Personal study
Students may also have to submit a personal study based on fieldwork or personal research that is approved by the exam board.

How is Archaeology taught and assessed?
Like many subjects, there will be much classroom work and reading from text books. But Archaeology is different in that it often involves visits to sites of archaeological interest where students can see for themselves the relevance of their subject. As mentioned above, students often have to complete a personal study, which can account for 20% of their final marks. The other marks are given according to performance in written exams.

Choosing other A level subjects to go with Archaeology
Other subjects that go well with Archaeology are History, Geography, Art, languages, Classical Civilisation, Latin and Classical Greek. But as with all subjects, there is no reason why students can't combine this with science-related or mathematically based subjects.

Archaeology at higher-education level

Archaeology is a well-established subject at higher-education level, even though it still remains a fairly specialised area. Students from this course gain both practical and analytical skills, so they have a lot to offer employers. You may not need an A level (or equivalent) in Archaeology to study it at HE level, but some institutions could want you to have an A level in History, Ancient History or Classical Civilisation.

A degree in Archaeology?

Archaeology degrees can vary quite a lot. Some are relatively 'modern' in their application of the practical skills of archaeology; others focus more on classical archaeology and its relationship with classical culture such as the arts, religion and literature. You have to decide what kind of archaeology you're most interested in. All courses will have elements of fieldwork, which students usually carry out during the Easter and summer vacations.

Combining Archaeology with other degree subjects

Archaeology figures quite highly in joint degrees, which allow you to concentrate on two allied disciplines. Common choices include:

- Architectural History and Archaeology
- Classics and Archaeology
- Geography and Archaeology
- Archaeology and Ethnography
- Archaeology and Social Anthropology.

Foundation degrees and HNDs

There are a few HNDs and Foundation degrees in Archaeology and related areas. These are useful for students who want to learn the vocational skills in the area rather than take a purely academic course.

Archaeology and your future career

Non-graduate jobs

The study of archaeology gives students a useful mix of both practical and intellectual skills. The skills of analysis, evaluation, ICT ability, weighing up evidence and making reasoned judgements are all useful in any job. There may be some assistant- or clerical-level work available in museums or galleries that may also require some archaeological skills and knowledge. Furthermore, some administrative positions, particularly in the Civil Service, demand the kinds of qualities mentioned above.

Graduate jobs directly related to Archaeology

Archaeologists can also be found in: national heritage agencies; local authorities; national parks; museums funded by national or local government; universities and colleges; archaeological societies; consultancies; and independent museums, trusts and charities. The main vocational areas related to this subject are:

» **Archaeologist**: works with or leads a team to plan and excavate, analyse finds and complete reports of findings.
» **Higher-education lecturer**: teaches Archaeology and carries out research activities in universities and some colleges of further education.

Graduate jobs in which a degree in Archaeology would be useful

» **Heritage manager**: conserves, interprets and promotes historic buildings and sites. Manages facilities at the site. Organises exhibitions and events, developing displays on the historic interest of the site.
» **Historic buildings inspector/conservation officer**: inspects and reports on buildings of special historic or architectural interest for purpose of preservation or long-term conservation.
» **Museum/art-gallery curator**: responsible for care and improvement of a collection including exhibitions, catalogues and organisation.
» **Museum education officer**: creates a link between a museum collection (or a number of museums) and the interests or needs of visitors. They are responsible for developing learning opportunities, which can be either informal or curriculum based.
» **Museum/gallery exhibitions officer**: responsible for activities and tasks associated with the planning and organising of permanent and travelling exhibitions. A pre-entry postgraduate qualification, such as an MA/Diploma in Museum Studies, is highly desirable.
» **Tourism officer**: promotes heritage as an attraction to incoming tourists, including marketing and promoting facilities, information provision and development of facilities.

Further information

Council for British Archaeology – www.britarch.ac.uk
Current Archaeology – www.archaeology.co.uk
English Heritage – www.english-heritage.org.uk

Art and Design, Applied

This course gives students a practical and theoretical understanding of art and design in a variety of contexts. It equips them with the skills to continue further study or training, or to move into employment within the art and design field. Students learn a range of creative techniques; at one end of the spectrum, this could be painting or drawing methods – at the other it could be how to create a 'practical' design for a new living space. One thing art and design students have in common is a visual appreciation of their environment; they will learn different ways of conveying that vision through different media including decorative arts, sculpture, graphic design, ceramics, textiles and photography.

From a theoretical point of view, students may also consider how art forms have developed over time and how they relate to their literary, social, and political contexts. GCE A/AS levels are also available in Graphic Design, Textiles, and Three-Dimensional Design.

Main elements of the course
The outline below is based on what the AQA exam board offers. For an exact definition of the AS and A2 syllabus you will be studying, you should consult your school or college or even the exam board itself.

» Art in the community
» Application and development of 2-D visual language
» Application and development of 3-D visual language
» Cultural and critical studies
» Drawing, painting or sculpture, and printmaking
» Graphic design
» Investigation of 2-D visual language

» Historical and contemporary contexts
» Investigation of 3-D visual language
» Photography and lens-based imagery
» Professional practice, communication and meaning
» Textile art and fashion
» Working to a brief
» Working to self-identified briefs
» 3-D design.

If possible, students should have studied Art (or Art and Design) at GCSE level or have taken a BTEC First Diploma in Art and Design, but this is not always required by schools and colleges.

How is Art and Design taught and assessed?

Although there may be some theoretical elements to the course, in essence Art and Design is very practical. You will be doing a lot of independent work in the art room or studio under the guidance of your teacher. Assessment is through a combination of producing portfolios of work and examinations. Candidates can choose to be assessed in one of four ways: AS single award (three units); AS double award (six units); A level single award (six units); A level double award (12 units).

Choosing other A level subjects to go with Art and Design

Most specialist courses at higher-education level require an A level in Art and Design as well as at least one other A level. Your choice of supporting A levels really depends on the kind of course, if any, you want to do afterwards. If you're interested in architecture, for instance, you may need A levels in Mathematics and ICT to help your applications; if you're interested in theatre design, choosing English Literature and Drama could help your cause. If, on the other hand, you want to work as an artist after your A levels, then choosing Business Studies or Accounting may also help your chances of long-term success.

Art and Design at higher-education level

Most people who go on to study Art and Design at higher-education level have completed a recent portfolio of work through a Foundation course at an art and design college. Most commonly, this is called a Diploma in Foundation Studies (Art and Design). Foundation courses are designed to give students an opportunity to experience a wider range of artistic media than they could at most schools. This also boosts their portfolio and enables them to make better applications for degree-level courses. For entry to most one-year Art Foundation courses, you need A level Art and Design and a portfolio of work at a high standard.

Remember: a Foundation course is a one-year programme designed to give students the necessary knowledge in a subject to prepare them for higher education. This is not the same as a Foundation degree. Foundation courses can be for any subject, but they are particularly common for Art and Design, where students need extra time to prepare a portfolio of work to get into higher education.

A degree in Art and Design?

Degree courses tend to specialise a bit more than any previous study and may split the whole field of Art and Design into specific degree programmes. The following are typical examples:

» BA (Hons) Fine Art
» BA (Hons) Textiles
» BA (Hons) Design
» BA (Hons) Fashion Studies.

Combining Art and Design with other degree subjects

Sometimes specific types of Art and Design degree programmes (such as those mentioned above) are combined together, but other popular combining subjects include: History of Art, Computing, Business Studies and Literature.

Foundation degrees and HNDs

Foundation degrees (not diplomas in foundation studies) do exist in Art and Design. Look at www.ucas.com and search under Foundation degrees. The Diploma in Foundation Studies (Art and Design) is a post-A level course that enables students to prepare for this subject at higher-education level. HNDs are available in Art and Design as well as Fine Art.

Art-and-Design A level and your future career

Non-graduate jobs

It's possible to get into some art-and-design-related jobs after A levels such as working as a junior design assistant in a creative design agency. Other work in which it's possible to get experience at this stage includes working as a marketing assistant and helping with the creative side of publications and promotions. Working as an assistant to a professional artist, photographer, designer or sculptor is also an option.

Graduate jobs related to Art and Design

Within art-and-design-related jobs, it is possible and quite common for a graduate to cross over to a discipline different from the one they studied, for example, fine art to graphic design. Related jobs include:

» **Arts administrator**: supports and generates artistic activity. The role may include marketing, promotion, book-keeping, finance and general administration. Appeals to those who want to combine working with art and people. Requires business and administration skills rather than creativity.

» **Exhibition/display designer**: organises the design of exhibition and display stands. Liaises with clients to produce designs that communicate their desired messages.

» **Fashion clothing designer**: produces designs for clothing and accessories. May specialise in an area such as sportswear.

» **Graphic designer**: produces visual solutions for the communication needs of clients. Needs creativity and imagination, good ICT skills and commercial awareness.

» **Illustrator**: produces illustrations for magazines, books, advertising, brochures, greetings cards, packaging, posters or newspapers. Specialisms include scientific, technical and medical illustrators.

» **Museum/gallery conservator/restorer**: preserves and cares for collections of artistic or cultural objects. Many specialise in one type of object, for example furniture. Good class of degree and some voluntary experience often necessary for entry.

» **Textile designer**: creates designs in knit, weave or print to be used in the production of fabric or textile products.

Graduate jobs in which a degree in Art and Design could be useful

» **Advertising art director**: creates visual ideas to be used in advertising. Works as part of a team alongside illustrators, photographers and those responsible for editorial. Can involve any media.

» **Art therapist**: works with people who present a variety of problems ranging from mental/physical illness, emotional and learning difficulties, stress and trauma. Aims to enable the client to effect change and growth on a personal level, within a safe environment, through the use of art materials.

» **Museum/art-gallery curator**: acquires, cares for, stores and presents a collection of artefacts or works of art in order to inform, educate and entertain the public. May include other elements such as public relations, fundraising and customer care.

» **Picture researcher/editor**: finds suitable images for print and electronic publications. Investigates copyright, negotiates fees, liaises with clients. Part-time and distance-learning courses are available.

» **Secondary-school teacher**: appeals to those who are interested in developing the skills and knowledge of others within the Art and Design curriculum. Secondary-school teaching mostly involves teaching Art, Design, Craft or Technology as part of the National Curriculum.

» **Visual merchandiser**: creates window and interior displays in shops and department stores with the aim of increasing sales.

Further information
Artists' Information Company – www.a-n.co.uk
Fashion jobs website – www.topfashionjobs.com
Your Creative Future (website with lots of information about creative careers) – www.yourcreativefuture.org.uk

Biology

Biology students learn about all life on the planet – human, plant and animal. One of the things that appeals to students who consider this subject is the sheer variety involved in the syllabus, ranging from how plants get their energy to how the human heart works to how biological systems relate to ecology and the environment. Some of the questions that A level biologists could be asked to consider include:

» What is the exact process of cell division in humans and animals?
» How does the human nervous system work in detail?
» How do viral and bacterial infections work and how does the immune system respond?
» What are ecosystems and how do they work?

Biology is a particularly popular subject at the moment because of prominent issues such as gene technology, the study of which is behind the advances in gene therapy now used by modern medicine. There may be some variation in topics according to the exam board used. Some, for instance, may put a greater emphasis on the social and environmental context of biology; all of them, however, cover the main core biological concepts. Students should be aware that GCE A/AS level in Human Biology is also offered by some exam boards.

Main elements of the course
The outline below is based on what the majority of exam-board syllabuses include. For an exact definition of the AS and A2 syllabus you will be studying, you should consult your school or college or even the exam board itself. This subject is also available at AEA level through AQA exam board.

Biological foundations
Cell structure and characteristics including an introduction to organelles; molecular biology, including the structure of lipids, carbohydrates and proteins; enzymes and how they work; cell membranes and the transport of substances in and out of cells; DNA and RNA; nuclear division; energy and ecosystems.

Human health and disease
Global patterns of disease distribution; diet and its effect on the body; gaseous exchange and exercise; smoking and disease; infectious diseases; immunity.

Transport and exchange
The mammalian transport system, the mammalian heart and transport in multicellular plants.

Key biological concepts
Energy and respiration; photosynthesis; populations and interactions; meiosis, genetics and gene control; classification, selection and evolution; control, co-ordination and homeostasis.

As well as these core subjects, exam boards will usually offer the following options:

- Growth development and reproduction
- The application of genetics
- Environmental biology
- Microbiology and technology
- Mammalian physiology and behaviour.

Students normally need at least a grade C in GCSE Biology or Science to take up A level Biology, as much of the syllabus requires some prior knowledge. Ability in Mathematics and Chemistry can also be useful; students will have to collect and manipulate data as well as understand the chemical processes that take place in the living world.

How is Biology taught and assessed?
Like many A2 and AS subjects, Biology is taught via a combination of class work and coursework. The class work involves making notes as the teacher talks, but much of it will be carrying out practical experiments in the laboratory. Some of these practicals will be assessed by the teacher and will form part of your final grade. Most Biology syllabuses involve an element of project work or coursework, which contributes to the final mark. The remainder of the grade is determined by written exams. For

some courses, there may also be some fieldwork, which could last anything from half a day to a week.

Choosing other A level subjects to go with Biology

Some degree courses require at least two science subjects, so check with higher-education institutions' entrance criteria before choosing which subjects to study alongside Biology. Common combinations include Biology, Physics (or Mathematics) and Chemistry but there is no reason why you should follow this pattern if other subjects appeal.

Biology at higher-education level

Biology at higher-education level is extremely popular and there are many different biology-related courses available, including biochemistry, biomedical science and genetics. Most of these related subjects would require A level Biology but there are a few exceptions. Those who have an interest in pursuing a career in medicine, dentistry and veterinary medicine usually take Biology at A level, although this is not always necessary.

A degree in Biology?

Like most degrees these days, Biology can be quite varied and flexible in its content. However, most degrees will comprise some core subjects (usually studied in the first year) and then the option of specialising in certain areas by choosing particular modules. Sometimes degrees in this area can be called Biological Sciences, often indicating a broader curriculum, but this is not always the case. Medical students can often do a degree in Biomedical Science or Biology as part of their five-year course. Always check the precise nature of the course before you take the plunge.

Combining Biology with other degree subjects

Biology can be combined with a whole range of subjects, not just those within the sciences. Common combinations include: Biology with Chemistry, Physics, Geography, Mathematics or Psychology. A word of warning: if you need a Biology degree for a particular job, try to check beforehand whether a combined Biology degree with another subject is acceptable.

Foundation degrees and HNDs

HNDs are seen as being on a level between A levels and a degree, and many institutions offer Biology at this level. It's often possible to convert to the degree programme after doing the diploma. In many cases, the diploma courses emphasise the practical, applied side of the subject, sometimes in relation to specific areas of work. This is also the case with some Foundation degrees in Biology, which have been designed in co-operation with organisations for which biological knowledge is directly useful, hence courses such as: Applied Biology, Botanical Conservation and Human Bioscience.

Biology and your future career

Non-graduate jobs
Many employers requiring A levels do not really mind which subjects applicants have. In that sense, Biology A level is as good a choice as any. However, there may be some non-graduate areas of work where Biology A level is still more useful than some others. These include:

» Healthcare jobs (including nursing training)
» Some forms of laboratory work (eg lab assistant in a school)
» Work as an assistant in a dental surgery
» Any job requiring attention to detail and practical skills.

It's also possible to start some scientific or biology-related jobs and do training on the job at a night class or with day release from work.

Graduate jobs directly related to Biology or Science
If you wish to use your degree directly there are several employment areas in which a degree in Biology is directly relevant. Some of the most popular jobs are listed below, but further study is often required.

» **Civil Service fast streamer**: employed by the Civil Service on the fast-stream development programme. Uses scientific knowledge to carry out research, develop policy, manage projects and provide general administration.
» **Clinical cytogeneticist**: provides an analytical interpretation and advice service to medical staff in hospitals.
» **Industrial science researcher**: an intellectually challenging role that can involve teamwork with other professionals, including those from other disciplines. Can involve developing new products, eg drugs, new processes.
» **Life science researcher**: employed in universities, health authorities and in certain industries (eg pharmaceutical, healthcare products, biotechnology). Investigates and analyses natural and living phenomena, gathering scientific information and generating knowledge.
» **Medical sales executive**: represents pharmaceutical companies to general practitioners, retail pharmacists and hospital doctors. Promotes pharmaceutical products in an ethical manner.

» **Scientific lab assistant**: helps scientists and others who are engaged in research, development, analysis or scientific investigations by carrying out a variety of technical and experimental tasks.
» **Secondary-school teacher**: teaches their own subject as a separate discipline and will also have a multidisciplinary approach through integrated science teaching.

Further information
To find out more about Biology as an A level, and science in general, visit the following websites:

Advanced Biology A level – www.advancedbiology.org
Institute of Biology – www.iob.org
NHS Careers – www.nhscareers.nhs.uk

Business Studies
(A level and Applied A level)

Students of business learn about organisations and how they work, as well as the different markets businesses serve. More often than not, business students will look at case studies from particular businesses and apply what they have learned to those case studies. The kinds of questions students of this subject could consider include:

» What factors make a business successful?
» What external influences affect organisations?
» What are the different ways of motivating staff?
» How do the different functions of finance, information and human resources work together?

In essence, students gain an understanding of how organisations operate and how to make effective business decisions.

Main elements of the course
The outline below is based on what the majority of exam-board syllabuses include. For an exact definition of the AS and A2 syllabus you will be studying, you should consult your school or college or even the exam board itself.

Business structures, objectives and external influences
How organisations are structured; internal processes; formulation of organisational objectives; how external influences affect objectives; staff motivation.

Marketing and production

How to identify and satisfy customer demand (including the use of market-research techniques); how to produce products of appropriate quality as efficiently as possible; analysing marketing data.

Financial management

Learning about financial management and accounting processes; the importance of effective budgeting; how to analyse the profitability and liquidity of a business; understanding cost and break-even analysis.

Analysis and decision making

How to analyse data from all areas of the business to make decisions; learning numerical techniques and analysis; learning how to apply these techniques to real business situations.

Business planning

Understanding the importance of planning and how to introduce it in all areas of the business; learning specific techniques of planning; how to identify organisational constraints and their effects on business planning cycles.

Corporate strategy

Understanding how strategy can shape the direction of an organisation; how strategy can respond to the external environment; developing a global strategy; using corporate strategy for managing change.

Applied A/AS level

Applied A level Business Studies has many of the same elements as the traditional GCE course, but there are three main differences: first, the applied course goes into more detail about some of the business functions/areas studied and how they can be applied in real life; second, students can take options with a more specialised vocational focus; and third, the assessment for the applied subject is based on producing portfolios of evidence rather than written exams.

As can be seen from the selection of modules below, the applied course is much more about 'how to do' business rather than its theoretical or historical origins. This outline is based on a sample from AQA, OCR and Edexcel:

- » Creating a marketing proposal
- » A business plan for the entrepreneur
- » Recruitment in the workplace
- » Managing and developing people

» Organising an event
» Career planning.

How is Business Studies taught and assessed?

A level
Like many subjects, there is a lot of classroom work, simply learning about the different areas of business as well as some of the analytical techniques. But this subject differs from some in that a lot of learning is conveyed through business case studies. Students look at real-life scenarios from the past and apply what they have learned to those situations. The assessment of this subject is done mainly by written exams but there is usually a significant piece of coursework to be done too, probably in the form of a business project.

Applied A level
The teaching of this course is similar to the traditional A level but there is a much more practice-based emphasis. Assessment is mainly by internally assessed portfolios of evidence with the occasional written exam. There are four possible routes for gaining an award in this subject: AS single award (three units); AS double award (six units); A level single award (six units); A level double award (12 units).

Choosing other A level/Applied subjects to go with Business Studies
In theory, you could combine Business Studies with any other subject, but popular choices include Mathematics, Computing, Accounting, Law, science subjects and Geography. One word of warning: if you want to study business at some of the more traditional universities, they may prefer more traditionally 'academic' A level subjects to some more 'modern' ones. Check their entry requirements before choosing.

Business Studies at higher-education level
Business is becoming an increasingly popular subject at higher-education level. The courses vary widely both in content and style. Some are very academically focused in that they examine the theories of management; others are much more vocationally focused in that their emphasis is on the practice of management and links with the business world. You have to ask yourself which type you would prefer.

A degree in Business Studies?
At a higher level, business-related courses can be called a variety of things: Management, Business Management, Business and Finance,

Business Operations and so on. Each course has a slightly different emphasis, so it's important to check the precise nature of each course. Most courses, however, include some core modules about business and management and then allow students to choose options over the last two years. Some courses even specify learning a foreign language as part of the course.

Combining Business Studies with other degree subjects

Popular combinations include: Business and Accounting, Business and Mathematics, Business and Law, Business and Psychology, and Business and Engineering. Most employers with a strong commercial focus aren't too bothered about how you combine your degree.

Foundation degrees and HNDs

There are many Foundation degree courses in Business and Business Management, as well as other business-related areas. Visit www.ucas.com for details of these. There are also many HND courses available in this area, including ICT Business, Business-related Law, E-commerce, Marketing and Human Resources.

Business Studies A level and your future career

Non-graduate jobs

This subject will give you an insight into the business world so employers may be more likely to take you on than those who have studied other subjects. Positions do exist in management and administration for those with A levels, especially specific programmes offered by companies in retail, banking, insurance and manufacturing.

Graduate jobs related to Business Studies

A knowledge of business is useful, if not essential, in most careers, so a list of these would be endless. When recruiting for commercial or financial job opportunities, employers are prepared to consider graduates in any subject but some give preference to a Business Studies background, whilst others refer to this as a definite requirement.

Graduate jobs in which a degree in Business Studies would be useful

Although the following occupations are open to graduates from any degree discipline, a Business Studies degree will provide useful background knowledge, evidence of some of the skills mentioned above and, possibly, some exemptions from papers in professional examinations.

- **Advertising account executive**: acts as a link between the client and the agency, taking responsibility for putting the proposal together and presenting it to the client. The executive co-ordinates the activities of the advertising team and administration.
- **Banking manager**: responsible for managing the daily business of a branch and for the development of new business, ensuring that sales targets are met and maintaining a customer-orientated retail team.
- **Chartered accountant**: provides financial information and maintains general accounting systems, performs audits and liaises with clients or management colleagues. Opportunities exist in industry, commerce, private practice and the public sector.
- **Distribution/logistics manager**: manages the supply, movement and storage of goods and materials. Plans, organises and co-ordinates material flow and storage through the process of manufacture from supplier to customer. Controls the total distribution operation.
- **Investment banker (corporate finance)**: advises private and corporate investors about their money and currency-related activities. Also seeks to promote related financial products appropriate to the clients' needs.
- **Management consultant**: provides a professional service to business, public and other undertakings by identifying and investigating problems concerned with strategy, policy, markets, organisation, procedures and methods.
- **Marketing executive**: promotes and sells products to the public. Works on various projects to support the brand/marketing manager in developing brands and promoting existing products.
- **Personnel officer**: develops and advises on all policies relating to human resources in an organisation.
- **Public-relations officer**: uses all forms of media and communications to project and protect the appropriate image of an organisation or individual.
- **Retail buyer**: successfully purchases attractive merchandise whose price, quality and availability meet customers' needs. Buyers must provide commercially viable merchandise ranges at competitive prices, whilst maximising profitability.
- **Retail manager**: in charge of the day-to-day management of a department or store; being responsible for staff, sales, customer service, effective cost control of stocks and resource management.
- **Sales executive**: promotes and maximises sales of a company's products or services in designated markets. Identifies new markets

and new business and acts as liaison between producer and the retailer or wholesaler.

Further information
Economics and Business Education Association – www.ebea.org.uk
Institute of Business Administration and Management – www.ibam.org
Institute of Chartered Secretaries and Administrators – www.icsa.org.uk
Rob Jones et al, *Business Studies*, Causeway Press, 2004

Chemistry

How can you test for the presence of acid? Why and how do substances change when you heat them? What are the properties of that changed substance? How do we express that change on paper? These are just some of the questions A level chemists have to think about. Some of these issues were considered at GCSE level, but A level goes into much more detail. Chemistry is about understanding the fundamental nature of life from a chemical point of view. Students learn the skills to work in a laboratory, acquire knowledge about the theories of chemistry and test some of those theories in practice.

Main elements of the course
The outline below is based on what the majority of exam-board syllabuses include. For an exact definition of the AS and A2 syllabus you will be studying, you should consult your school or college or even the exam board itself. This subject is available at AEA level through AQA exam board.

Structures, bonding and the main chemical 'groups'
Most courses go into depth about atomic structure, chemical formulae, chemical bonding and groups of chemicals such as Group 7 (chlorine to iodine).

Organic and inorganic chemistry; energetics; kinetics; qualitative equilibria
Includes: introduction to alkanes, alkenes, alcohols and halogenoalkanes; industrial inorganic chemistry; chemical reactions (endothermic and exothermic); calculating the rates of chemical reactions; understanding the dynamic nature of chemical equilibria.

Laboratory chemistry
This is all about the process of carrying out chemistry in the lab and students developing their experimental skills. Assessing a student's practical skills in the lab forms an important part of every A level course.

Periodicity, quantitative equilibria and functional group chemistry
More advanced theories about chemical reactions; understanding chemical properties of certain parts of the periodic table; acids and bases; further organic chemistry (including acids, esters, carbonyl, nitrogen compounds).

Transition metals, quantitative kinetics and applied organic chemistry
Oxidisation; ionic bonding; reaction mechanisms and aromatic compounds; understanding rates of chemical reactions using quantitative techniques; learning tests to identify certain organic compounds; identifying certain chemical structures of organic compounds; using a spectrometer; understanding the importance of organic chemistry in relation to agriculture, the pharmaceutical business and other materials.

How is A level Chemistry taught and assessed?
Chemistry students learn both the theory and practice of the subject, therefore they spend lots of time learning in a lab, observing practical demonstrations and carrying out supervised experiments. Depending on whether the subject is taken at AS or A2 level, exams will be taken at different points during the course. Most will be written exams but there will also be an assessed practical examination. As well as being practical, a good head for figures is also helpful to do well at this subject.

Choosing other A level subjects to go with Chemistry
Many students choose to combine this subject with Biology, Physics or Mathematics. The reason for this is that acceptance onto some degree courses requires at least two science subjects at A level. If that isn't relevant to you, then there's no reason why you can't combine Chemistry with any other subject.

Chemistry at higher-education level
Chemistry at higher-education level is extremely popular and there are many different Chemistry-related courses available, including Biochemistry, Medical Biochemistry, Chemical Physics and many others. Most of these related subjects would require A level Chemistry but there are a few exceptions. Those who have an interest in pursuing a career in medicine, dentistry or veterinary medicine usually take Chemistry at A level, although this is not always necessary.

A degree in Chemistry?

Like most degrees these days, Chemistry can be quite varied and flexible in its content. However, most degrees will have some core subjects (usually studied in the first year) and then have the option of allowing students to specialise in certain areas by choosing particular modules. Most degree courses expand upon the areas studied at A level and teaching involves a combination of set lectures, small group tutorials, assigned coursework and, of course, work in the laboratory.

Combining Chemistry with other degree subjects

Chemistry at degree level will have some overlap with other sciences. Even so, students often combine this subject with Biology or Physics. Other joint degree programmes offered by universities include:

» Chemistry with Mathematics
» Chemistry with a European language
» Chemistry with Management
» Medicinal Chemistry.

Foundation degrees and HNDs

There are Foundation degrees in Chemistry, Chemical Technology and Chemical Sciences and in vocational areas such as Forensic Science. It is also possible to do an HND in Applied Chemistry, in which the emphasis is very much on the practical applications of chemistry for today.

Chemistry and your future career

Non-graduate jobs

Most jobs using chemistry require higher qualifications. It may be possible, however, to get some experience working as a lab assistant, dental assistant or veterinary assistant, but these often require further training too. Having said that, the subject is highly regarded by employers in lots of different areas of work so students needn't limit themselves to chemistry-related occupations.

Graduate jobs directly related to Chemistry

» **Analytical chemist**: performs structural, quantitative, product and formulation analyses using state-of-the-art techniques, often in support of other scientists.
» **Biomedical scientist (MLSO)**: carries out laboratory investigations on human samples necessary for the diagnosis, treatment and prevention of illness or disease.

» **Colour technologist**: produces dyes and pigments for the colouration of products such as textiles, paper, cosmetics and foodstuffs for highly sensitive biomedical applications and dye lasers.
» **Industrial research scientist**: organises and carries out systematic investigations to develop new products or improve existing products to meet consumer demand for quality, safety and price.
» **Materials engineer**: conducts technical investigations related to the development and production of a wide range of materials, eg glass, metals, polymers and plastics.
» **Process-development scientist**: scales up processes developed in the laboratory so that they may be used in manufacturing large quantities. The aim is to produce products for the market in an efficient, economical and safe way.
» **Product-development scientist**: takes ideas or discoveries generated by research, then develops or formulates them to the point where new products can be manufactured. The work may be to develop new products or to improve the performance of existing ones.
» **Quality-assurance officer**: develops and applies tests to ensure raw materials, intermediates and finished products meet specified standards of composition, texture, taste, appearance and performance.
» **Research scientist (physical sciences)**: plans and conducts experimental research, evaluates ideas, uses and develops theoretical knowledge in either theoretical or applied areas.
» **Secondary-school teacher, further-education lecturer, or higher-education lecturer**: teaches Chemistry in schools or colleges of further education. Lecturers in higher education balance their teaching load with research and supervision of postgraduate researchers.

Graduate jobs in which a degree in Chemistry could be useful

» **Clinical biochemist**: carries out tests on samples from patients to assist with the investigation, diagnosis and treatment of disease. Liaises with clinicians on interpretation of results.
» **Forensic scientist**: analyses samples in relation to crime. Writes reports which are presented as evidence in courts.
» **(Medical) sales executive**: negotiates sales and generates new business between producers and their clients, either business to general public or, more likely, business to business.
» **Patent agent**: acts as an agent for inventors or companies with new ideas or processes to protect the intellectual property for the client.
» **Scientific journalist**: researches and writes scientific news and articles for the general public or for more specialist audiences.

» **Toxicologist**: carries out and interprets laboratory and field studies to identify toxins and their effect on living systems and the environment.

Further information

Chemistry and Industry magazine online – www.chemind.org
Chemsoc careers – www.chemsoc.org.uk
Royal Society of Chemistry – www.rsc.org

Classical Civilisation

This subject is about the civilisations of Ancient Rome and Greece. It allows students who don't have knowledge of the Greek and Latin languages to gain an appreciation of culture during the period 1500 BC to AD 450. To study Classical Civilisation means to study the politics, art, philosophy and literature of the time and geographical settings.

Main elements of the course
The outline below is based on what the majority of exam-board syllabuses include. For an exact definition of the AS and A2 syllabus you will be studying, you should consult your school or college or even the exam board itself.

Greek and Roman literature (epics, tragedy, comedy and satire)
A great emphasis is given to the literature of the time including:

» The *Iliad*, *Odyssey* and Virgil's *Aeneid* (Greek and Roman epics)
» The works of Aeschylus, Sophocles and Euripides (Greek tragedy)
» The works of Aristophanes, Horace, Juvenal and Pliny (Greek comedy and Roman satire).

Greek and Roman history
As well as literature, students are asked to consider the historical writings of the time, including:

» The works of Herodotus and Thucydides (Greek)
» The writings of Tacitus and Suetonius (Roman).

There is usually some emphasis on the Roman occupation of Britain and written evidence about it.

Greek art and architecture
Students learn how to assess the importance of Greek art and architecture and how it reflects the society of its time.

Approaches to archaeology and Roman sites and artefacts
In this module students learn the definition of archaeology, archaeological methods and practice, archaeological principles and how to interpret archaeological evidence. They also learn about artefacts originating from Roman Britain.

How is A level Classical Civilisation taught and assessed?
Students learn by examining a range of writing (usually in translation) from the period in question. There may be some opportunities to visit a Roman or Greek site of archaeological interest. Most of the assessment is carried out by written exams over the two years but there is also a coursework option as well.

Choosing other A level subjects to go with Classical Civilisation
This A level overlaps with many disciplines and combines well with Literature, Ancient History, Philosophy, Archaeology, History and many others. But, like most subjects, it can be combined with any other subjects, including the sciences.

Classical Civilisation at higher-education level
There may be some courses called Classical Civilisation at higher level but most will probably be called Classics or Classical Studies. For entry to an HE course, an A level in Classics or Classical Civilisation is not normally needed, but good grades in traditional arts and/or humanities subjects would stand you in good stead.

A degree in Classics/Classical Civilisation?
Like A level Classical Civilisation, the focus of most degree courses will be on ancient Roman and Greek history and civilisation. However, this will be much more wide ranging and studied in much more depth. There may also be a requirement for students to become familiar with written Greek and Latin so that they can analyse historical documents in the original language.

Combining Classics with other degree subjects

Classics cuts across quite a few disciplines so it's quite common to see it combined with other subjects. Some joint programmes offered by universities include:

» Classical Studies and French
» Classical Studies and Philosophy
» Classics and Applied Computing
» War Studies and Classical Studies
» Classical Studies with Film Studies.

These are just a few examples: there are many other possible combinations.

Foundation degrees and HNDs

Currently there is no separate Classical Studies Foundation degree, but you may be interested in some courses that include elements of History or Archaeology. Similarly, there is currently no HND available in this subject.

Classical Studies and your future career

Non-graduate jobs

This A level will give you lots of marketable skills for a variety of jobs, even though you probably won't be able to use the specific knowledge you've learned. Skills you can gain from this course include the ability to research, form judgements, analyse information and empathise.

Graduate jobs directly related to Classics

There are only a few jobs that are directly related to a Classics degree. For the following occupation a degree in a classical subject is essential.

■ **Secondary-school Classics teacher**: there are a few Postgraduate Certificate in Education (PGCE) courses for graduates wanting to teach Classics in state secondary schools. Opportunities also exist in primary schools, independent schools, sixth-form colleges and further or higher education.

Graduate jobs in which Classics could be useful

Jobs in which the transferable skills learned from a Classics background are particularly useful include:

» **Administration**: planning and organising services, providing information and collecting data to form the basis for future actions within the organisation, informing the world outside the organisation. You could work in public service, industry (company secretary), education, health service, charities, voluntary or international organisations.

» **Archivist**: reserves, stores and safeguards records for permanent retention. Makes records accessible for administrative or historical research purposes. Latin is necessary for work with older archives.

» **Civil Service fast streamer**: involves policy making (administrative trainee) or general management (staffing, finance, immigration, consular work) roles within embassies or high commissions abroad, and in the Foreign and Commonwealth Office in London.

» **Museum/art-gallery curator**: the collection, documentation, preservation, display and interpretation of materials for public benefit.

» **Solicitor**: prepares deeds and contracts of all types, manages legal cases, instructs counsel (ie barristers) in the higher courts and acts as an advocate for others in the lower courts. You could work in private practice as a generalist or specialist, in industry, public service, law centres, magistrates courts or the armed services.

» **Technical author**: preparing technical information for publication in a way that is intelligible to a wide range of users. You need to produce clear, logical, unambiguous and accurate text. You must be able to communicate effectively with very different people from engineers to school children.

Further information

Council for British Archaeology – www.britarch.ac.uk
Current Archaeology – www.archaeology.co.uk
Institute for Conservation – www.icon.org.uk

Communication Studies

How do we communicate effectively? How are social values communicated through TV programmes such as soap operas? Is the meaning behind a form of communication, eg a newspaper story, solely dependent on the intentions of the writer? These are some of the questions that A level students of Communication Studies consider. The formal study of this subject is about the theory and practice of communications and, given the way technology has affected the way we communicate, this subject is more interesting than ever.

Main elements of the course

The outline below is based on what the majority of exam-board syllabuses include. For an exact definition of the AS and A2 syllabus you will be studying, you should consult your school or college or even the exam board itself.

Communication practice

This module looks at the theory and practice of personal communication skills with a particular emphasis on oral communication.

Texts and meanings in communication

In this unit students are encouraged to think about how meaning is conveyed through communication in different ways and through different media. Students develop skills in critical-reading techniques.

Themes in personal communication

Students are introduced to different perspectives of personal communication, including interpersonal communication, non-verbal communication and communication in groups.

Culture, context and communication
This module focuses on concepts such as communication within a culture, on ideology, the mass media and in specific environments.

Issues in communication
This is an opportunity for students to explore in depth some of the controversies in relation to theories of personal and cultural communications as well as the links between them. One such issue could be the impact of new technologies.

How is A level Communication Studies taught and assessed?
There is a lot of classroom theory, but this subject may involve students using media such as websites, film and TV footage, newspaper archives and other means of communication. Assessment is by a mixture of written exams and practical work such as an assessed presentation and/or project.

Choosing other A level subjects to go with Communication Studies
Communication Studies obviously lends itself to being combined with subjects such as English Literature, Drama, Media Studies, History and Sociology, but it can be combined with almost any subject. It's still a relatively new A level so, if you hope to go on to higher education, make sure it is seen as an acceptable subject in terms of entrance criteria for degree courses.

Communication Studies at higher-education level
Studying communication at HE level involves understanding further the media of communication (eg TV, print, the web), the 'codes' of communication (eg language and visual symbols), the ways that people interact (eg conversation and mass-level communication) and the contexts and purposes of communication. You will go into more depth than you did at A level and be much more analytical in your approach.

A degree in Communication Studies?
It is sometimes possible to specialise in a particular type of Communication Studies, such as mass media or the internet, but degree courses are usually broad rather than narrow. Some modules from a typical degree course include the following:

» Interpersonal communication
» Media sociology

» Social impacts of communication technologies
» Digital communication
» Theoretical issues: Marxism, feminism and postmodernism
» Communication and racism.

Combining Communication Studies with other degree subjects

Subjects that can be combined well with this subject include: English, Media Studies, Philosophy, History, Sociology, Linguistics and Politics.

Foundation degrees and HNDs

There are Foundation degrees in Communication at Work and Communication in Organisations. There are also some related to Media Studies, of which Communication Studies forms an important part. Currently there is no HND in Communication Studies available in England, but in Scotland HNDs in Communication and Media and in Communication Studies are available.

Communication Studies and your future career

Non-graduate jobs

An A level in Communication Studies will give you skills in communicating effectively, the ability to analyse issues and critically evaluate pieces of writing, and an awareness of popular culture. These skills may enable you to get junior positions in advertising, marketing, public relations, the media and other areas of business.

Graduate jobs related to Communication/Media Studies

Many students on these courses are interested in gaining employment in all aspects of the media industry. Careers in the media, however, are highly sought after and competition is likely to be fierce.

■ **Broadcast assistant, radio**: assists with production and presentation of programmes for local and national radio stations.
» **Broadcasting presenter**: fronts the programme; specific responsibilities vary depending on the programme.
» **Journalism**: reports on news and other areas of interest for newspapers, periodicals, radio and TV.
» **Multimedia programmer**: researches, develops and produces materials for new-media-based company activities.

» **Programme researcher, broadcasting/film/video**: acts as an assistant producer with responsibility for conception and implementation of a programme.
» **Radio producer**: responsible for initiating ideas, selling these to commissioning editors and managing the technical and creative team to produce the final programme.
» **Television/film/video producer**: undertakes the artistic interpretation of materials and directs the production of shows/films.
» **Television production assistant**: provides organisational and secretarial services for programme director.

Graduate jobs in which Communication Studies could be useful

» **Advertising account executive**: takes overall responsibility for co-ordination, planning and organisation of advertising campaigns.
» **Editorial assistant**: assists editorial staff in the commissioning, planning and production of books, journals and magazines.
» **Event organiser**: identifies potential business, researches, writes, plans and runs all types of conference on behalf of a client or own organisation.
» **Information officer/manager**: ensures effective communication of information relating to a particular field of interest.
» **Market research executive**: undertakes systematic research to determine the potential market for a product or service.
» **Public-relations account executive**: PR agencies work for their clients in presenting their image to the public. They decide on strategies to be used and which media would be the most effective.

Further information
Dimbleby and Burton, *More than Words: An Introduction to Communication*, Routledge
Fiske, John, *An Introduction to Communication Studies*, Routledge
Skillset – www.skillset.org; www.skillsformedia.com

Computing

Computers are more central to our lives than ever before. Students of A level Computing will not only get a better understanding of how computers work but will also look at how computers and information systems are used to solve organisational problems and how they are used in other areas of life. How do you design and implement a computer system? What's the most appropriate ICT application for this situation? These are just some of the questions that students of this subject are asked to consider.

Main elements of the course

The outline below is based on what the majority of exam-board syllabuses include. For an exact definition of the AS and A2 syllabus you will be studying, you should consult your school or college or even the exam board itself. Students taking the AS award only will have to study about 50% of the modules needed for the full A2 award.

Computer systems

In this module students learn about the many different applications of computer systems; the social, legal and economic implications of ICT; the different types of data files and data security; software and hardware; networking and maintenance.

Design and organisation of information systems

Students learn about what constitutes an information system; whether an information system is suitable for computerisation; organising data; designing and implementing software.

Computer systems designs
Understanding databases; organising files; understanding hardware and software; networks and communications

Systems development
Different ways of implementing an information system; project management; managing information; data structures; programming.

How is A level Computing taught and assessed?
Case studies make up much of the teaching methods of this course – students work with them to generate ICT-based solutions for business problems or scenarios. Students usually have to do two projects (one at AS stage and the other at A2 stage), probably on system design and/or software development. The rest of the assessment is by written exams at various points in the course. Although you don't need your own computer (your school or college should have them), it will help when it comes to independent work at home.

Choosing other A level subjects to go with Computing
Subjects chosen to combine with computing include Mathematics, Management, Business, Law, Accounting and many others. Bear in mind that you may not need Computing A level to study it at degree level.

Computing and ICT at higher-education level
There are very many ICT-related courses available at higher-education level. Some are very theoretical; others are very practical or applied in their emphasis. 'Computer Science' tends to be more academic and theoretical whereas 'Computer Studies' tends to be more practical. You should always check the specific nature of a course before applying.

A degree in Computing?
Most computing courses, even if they are theoretical, will consider how ICT is applied to business, industry and research. There are usually core components in the first year with some flexibility in the final two years, depending on your interests. The kinds of issues considered include:

» Web and internet technologies
» Object-orientated software engineering
» Object-orientated modelling
» Communications and networks
» Logic programming
» Bioinformatics
» Information security
» Computational finance.

Assessment is by a combination of final exams, coursework and project work.

Combining Computing degrees with other degree subjects

There are numerous possible combinations, but joint programmes offered by some ICT/Computer Science university departments include:

» Computer Science with Management
» Computer Science with French
» Computer Science with Artificial Intelligence
» Computer Science and Physics
» Computer Science and Mathematics.

Foundation degrees and HNDs

There are many Foundation degrees in ICT-related subjects, examples being Business Information Technology, Web Development and Design for Digital Technologies. Find a course at www.ucas.com. There are also a number of options at HND level which could be worth exploring.

Computing and your future career

Non-graduate jobs

Given that nearly every organisation needs computers now, you will be an asset if you have an advanced understanding of them. In that sense, there are quite a few junior positions that you could apply for. You may even be able to get work in ICT support in some organisations without any further qualifications.

Graduate jobs directly related to Computing

» **Applications developer**: writes and modifies programs to enable a computer to carry out specific tasks, such as stock control or payroll, typically for technical, commercial and business users.
» **Database administrator**: responsible for the usage, accuracy, efficiency, security, maintenance and development of an organisation's computerised databases.
» **Information-technology consultant**: gives independent and objective advice on how best to use information technology to solve business problems. The work includes analysing problems, making recommendations and implementing new systems.
» **Software engineer**: specifies, develops, documents and maintains computer software programs in order to meet client or employer needs. Usually works as part of a team.

» **Systems designer**: takes the specification for the requirements of a computer system and designs the system including hardware, software, communications, installation, testing and maintenance.
» **Systems developer**: sets up the computer operating systems and standard software services essential to the operation of any computer.

Graduate jobs in which Computing and ICT would be useful

The following jobs will make some use of your ICT background.

» **ICT sales professional**: sells computer hardware, software and peripherals; normally works in conjunction with sales representatives for a computer manufacturer.
» **Magazine journalist**: researches and writes news and feature articles which are suited to the magazine's reader profile.
» **Recruitment consultant**: particularly for the ICT sector. Brings together jobseekers with vacancies on behalf of an employer.
» **Secondary-school teacher**: teaches one or more specialist subject/s to classes of secondary pupils aged 11–18. ICT is currently a shortage subject.

Further information
British Computer Society – www.bcs.org
Computer Information Center – www.compinfo-center.com
Heathcote, Pat, *A Level Computing*, Payne-Gallway, 2004

Design and Technology (Product Design)

Students of this subject learn all about the ways products in society are designed, created and implemented. At one end of the spectrum this may involve the creative and artistic design process; at the other it may be design and technology in an industrial context. Students also gain a critical understanding of the influences of design and technology processes from a historical perspective and in current practice. In particular, the use of Information Technology is also emphasised as a way of enhancing design and technology processes. As a student of A level Design and Technology, you will also be encouraged to use your own creativity and innovative skills to produce your own high-quality products.

Some exam boards offer A levels in different aspects of Design and Technology such as Fashion and Textiles, Food Technology, Resistant Materials Technology and Systems Control Technology.

Main elements of the course
The outline below is based on what the majority of exam-board syllabuses include. For an exact definition of the syllabus you will be studying, you should consult your school or college or even the exam board itself.

Industrial and commercial products and practices
Learning how to create design specifications; understanding the different characteristics of a range of materials; large-scale manufacturing processes; quality control; estimating the potential appeal of a product; health and safety issues.

Product development
Students have to complete independent project work in relation to developing a product.

Materials, components and systems
Classification of materials (eg ferrous and non-ferrous) and components (eg rivets, nuts, bolts, etc); preparing and testing materials; computer-aided design (CAD); the use of ICT in the manufacturing process.

Design and technology capability
This is a synoptic unit in which students have to make connections from all they've learned so far. The particular emphasis is on the step-by-step process of creating a workable and marketable design and product.

How is A level Design and Technology taught and assessed?
This subject is taught by a mixture of teacher-led activities and 'hands-on' practical work. Students have to work to design briefs and produce portfolios and projects throughout the two years. The amount depends on whether you are an AS or A2 candidate. At least 40% of the assessment marks are based on practical coursework and the rest will be assessed by written exams at various points in the course. To do well in this subject you will need a practical mind, good business sense and creative flair.

Choosing other A level subjects to go with Design and Technology
There are many possibilities. Those with an artistic bent could choose A levels in the creative field and those who are more interested in the technical side could consider subjects such as Engineering, Computing and Manufacturing, which are all offered at A level and/or Applied A level.

Design and Technology at higher-education level
Those with an A level in this subject could be drawn to a whole range of higher-education courses such as Architecture, Product Design, Engineering and IT. Courses in Design and Technology have different emphases but most have strong links with industry, with some offering a sandwich placement as part of the course. Art or Technology-related A levels/Applied A levels are usually preferred but not essential.

A degree in Design and Technology?
Like many courses, this tends to include core courses and some optional ones in Years 2 and 3. Some of the following modules may appear in university courses:

» Design practice
» Materials science and processing

» Computing for designers
» Electronic systems
» Design for sustainable development
» Management and marketing
» Internet and interface for designers
» Computer-aided modelling
» Universal design.

Combining Design and Technology with other degree subjects

Many courses in Design and Technology have different focuses (eg computer-aided design, engineering product design, product design and management and so on). This may affect the subjects that students would like to combine with design and technology.

Foundation degrees and HNDs

There are Foundation degrees in specific areas of Design and Technology, especially in relation to creative arts and design and engineering. Visit www.ucas.com to find one. While there are no specific HNDs in Design and Technology, they do exist in 3-D Design and Graphic Design.

Design and Technology and your future career

Non-graduate jobs

Apprenticeships are a possibility in construction, manufacturing or engineering. It may also be possible to get junior positions (technician level) in computer-aided design or engineering.

Graduate jobs related to Design and Technology

» **Exhibition/display designer**: organises the design of exhibition and display stands. Liaises with clients to produce designs that communicate their desired messages.
» **Fashion clothing designer**: produces designs for clothing and accessories. May specialise in an area such as sportswear.
» **Production engineer**: planning, managing and maintaining production methods and processes to make the most efficient use of resources.
» **Production manager**: organising and scheduling production, selecting and controlling process variables, setting and meeting targets, and people management.
» **Quality-assurance officer**: establishing and operating systems that ensure quality standards in products, packing, delivery, labelling, etc. Also involves trouble-shooting and technical investigations.

» **Technical sales engineer**: technical advisory work, sales and after-sales service.
» **Textile designer**: creates designs in knit, weave or print to be used in the production of fabric or textile products.

Graduate jobs in which a degree in Design and Technology could be useful

» **Advertising art director**: creates visual ideas to be used within advertising. Works as part of a team alongside illustrators, photographers and those responsible for editorial. Can involve any media.
» **Information scientist**: finding, storing, evaluating and disseminating scientific, technical and commercial information.
» **Information technology and management services** (industrial engineering, work study, ICT, systems, etc): investigating business, commercial and industrial problems and data-processing requirements.

Further information

Design Council – www.designcouncil.org.uk
E. Norman et al, *Advanced Design and Technology*, Longman

Drama and Theatre Studies

As a student of A level Drama and Theatre Studies you will have the opportunity to develop your performance skills in many different areas. You will also gain a greater understanding of how playwrights use certain techniques to enable their plays to come to life on the stage. The skills gained while studying this course will give a good start for a career in the theatre, but equally it is a good all-round subject for those who simply want to deepen their interest in and enjoyment of the area.

Main elements of the course

Edexcel, AQA and WJEC currently offer this A level, although OCR offers a course in Performance Studies. For an exact definition of the AS and A2 syllabus you will be studying, you should consult your school, college or the exam board itself. The following outline is based largely on the Edexcel syllabus.

Unit 1: exploration of drama and theatre

You study two plays chosen by your school or college.

Unit 2: text in performance I

You will be examined on your acting or design skills within a directed production of a play.

Unit 3: text in context I

You will have to demonstrate your understanding of the play used in Unit 2 as well as another seen in performance.

Unit 4: devising

Students learn how to devise an original piece of theatre for presentation to an audience.

Unit 5: text in performance II
Here you will study a further play in depth from the viewpoint of a designer, director or performer.

Unit 6: text in context II
This unit requires the study of two prescribed plays in detail. You will have to examine the plays from different points of view and make connections between them, building on what you've learned from the previous units.

Students who intend to complete the full AS and A2 course complete all six modules. Those taking only the AS complete the first three modules.

How is A level Drama and Theatre Studies taught and assessed?
There is some classroom learning as part of the course, but you will also be spending a lot of time doing practical performance work, possibly in a drama studio. A good grade in GCSE English Literature would help you with this course but it's not always a prerequisite. Assessment is by a combination of written exams, coursework and assessed performances.

Choosing other A level subjects to go with Drama and Theatre Studies
Good companions for this subject include English Literature, Media Studies, History and perhaps Applied Performing Arts. Be aware of any overlaps between subjects and check the admissions criteria of universities if you want to study at a higher level.

Drama and Theatre Studies at higher-education level
There are many different types of Theatre Studies-related courses out there. Some specialise in particular aspects of drama and theatre such as performance, directing, stage design, lighting and so on. Others go for a broad overview of drama and the theatre. You have to ask yourself which one would suit you more. Some courses include a year abroad at another university.

A degree in Drama and Theatre Studies?
Some sample degree modules from a typical degree programme in this area might include:

» Writing and performance
» Staging histories
» Critical theories

» Elements of performance
» Explorations in space
» Practical skills.

Combining Drama and Theatre Studies with other degree subjects

This subject is often offered in combination with English Literature, a modern language, History, Media Studies and many more.

Foundation degrees and HNDs

There are HNDs in specific areas of the theatre and performing arts. There are also a number of Foundation degree courses in many different aspects of performing arts. You can search for them at www.ucas.com.

Drama and Theatre Studies and your future career

Non-graduate jobs

If you want a career in performance or in the technical side of the theatre, you will probably have to do further study. It's possible to get your foot in the door straight after your A levels, though, by working in an administrative role in a theatre, for example in the box office.

Graduate jobs related to Drama and Theatre Studies

The availability of some of the following jobs may depend on the type of degree you've done and relevant work experience. Some related jobs will require relevant postgraduate study and if you want to become a performer you may need further professional training.

» **Actor**: using speech, body language and movement, an actor communicates a character and situations to an audience.
» **Dramatherapist**: using drama to treat or educate people with health or emotional difficulties through therapeutic techniques.
» **Secondary-school teacher**: teaching drama, music or other curriculum subjects in schools and colleges.
» **Theatre director**: co-ordinates all the artistic aspects of a dramatic presentation from inception, through production stages and rehearsals, to the final performance.
» **Theatre stage manager**: organises and co-ordinates rehearsals and performances, and liaises between the director and the technical staff.
» **Wardrobe manager**: supervises making, buying, hiring and maintenance of costumes, accessories and wigs, and controls the budget for all these items.

Graduate jobs in which a degree in Drama and Theatre Studies could be useful

» **Arts administrator**: facilitates the planning and promotion of visual and performing-arts activities, sometimes specialising in areas such as finance and marketing.
» **Community arts worker**: concerned with the promotion of the arts in the community, often through working with young people in schools and youth centres.
» **Journalist**: there are many specialist publications covering the arts, but entry is very competitive. Graduates could start in mainstream broadcast or print journalism and specialise or become freelance later.
» **Programme researcher**: supports the producer by helping to organise and plan the programme.
» **Television production assistant**: organises and co-ordinates programme activities, booking performers and facilities and providing administrative support.

Further information
Equity (Actors' Union) – www.equity.org.uk
National Association of Youth Theatres – www.nayt.org.uk
National Council for Drama Training – www.ncdt.co.uk

Economics

As a student of A level Economics, you will learn about how the markets work, what factors affect them and make them crash or fail. You will also consider how economies develop, the place of the UK in the global market and how economies are managed by countries. On a more specific level, students may consider how economic forces affect things such as house prices, petrol prices and the price of a range of consumable goods. Students become familiar with concepts such as inflation, balance of payments and the pros and cons of a single European currency.

Main elements of the course

The outline below is based on what the majority of exam-board syllabuses include. For an exact definition of the syllabus you will be studying, you should consult your school or college or even the exam board itself. This subject is also available at AEA level through the AQA exam board.

Your course will cover most or all of the following:

- » Markets – how they work
- » Markets – why they fail
- » Managing the economy
- » Industrial economics
- » Economic development
- » Labour markets
- » The UK in the global economy.

How is A level Economics taught and assessed?

Much of the subject is classroom-based and teacher-led, but students may also consider case studies and TV programmes, and analyse newspaper reports, charts, graphs and tables. Students should have a good head for figures and possess good analytical skills. A good grade in GCSE Mathematics will help you in this area. Assessment is mainly by written exam at various points in the course, although there may be some element of coursework too.

Choosing other A level subjects to go with Economics

Popular choices to combine with Economics include History, Mathematics, Computing and Management/Business, but like most subjects it can be combined with any A level discipline.

Economics at higher-education level

Some degree courses are very mathematical, so A level Mathematics will be just as useful as A level Economics if you want to do a degree in the subject. The most prestigious courses, such as the one offered by the London School of Economics (LSE), will demand the very highest A level grades to get a place. Having said that, Economics is a subject offered by many institutions, so it should be possible to get a place with lower grades.

A degree in Economics?

There is some variation in Economics degrees around the country but most of them have some common core subjects, including:

» Mathematical methods
» Elementary statistical theory
» Microeconomic principles
» Macroeconomic principles
» Principles of econometrics.

There may also be some optional papers in the second and/or third year, such as:

» Managerial accounting
» Africa and the world economy
» Locational change and business activity
» Europe and the global economy
» The politics of international economic relations
» Further mathematical methods (calculus)
» Game theory
» Operational research methods
» Philosophy of economics.

Combining Economics with other degree subjects
Very well-known combinations include: Philosophy, Politics and Economics (PPE), Economics with History, Mathematics and Economics, Business Management with Economics, and Economics with Law. Economics with a foreign language is also becoming more common. If you intend to work as an economist, however, it's probably safer in career terms to do pure Economics.

Foundation degrees and HNDs
There are no Foundation degrees specifically in Economics but there are some in Business Administration and Management, which may overlap with elements of Economics. Similarly, while there are HNDs in Business, there are none purely in Economics.

Economics and your future career

Non-graduate jobs
A level Economics is highly regarded by employers and should stand you in good stead should you decide to start your career without going on to further study. Banks, retail organisations, insurance companies and some areas of the City and financial services take on people with good A levels, although some jobs require a degree.

Graduate jobs related to Economics
The role of economist is probably the most obvious work area directly related to your course. Most economists are concerned with practical applications of economic policy. They use their understanding of economic relationships to advise businesses and other organisations, including insurance companies, banks, securities firms, industry and trade associations, unions and government agencies. Entry to the profession is very competitive. Successful candidates tend to have a strong academic record and, often, a higher degree as well.

Graduate jobs in which a degree in Economics could be useful

» **Accountancy**: providing financial information and maintaining general accounting systems, performing audits and liaising with clients or management colleagues. Opportunities exist in industry, commerce, private practice and the public sector.
» **Actuarial work**: assessing probabilities and risk, traditionally in the insurance and pensions sectors, although increasingly in other areas. Requires strong mathematical and statistical skills.

» **Corporate, commercial and investment banking**: providing a broad range of financial services and advice to companies, institutions and governments. This includes dealing with mergers and acquisitions; arranging or underwriting equity or debt issues; identifying and securing new deals with clients.

» **Insurance underwriter**: assesses risks and premiums to be charged, liaises with clients and brokers. Other insurance industry roles, such as broking, claims and sales are likely to involve more client contact.

» **Investment analyst**: undertakes research to provide ideas and information to fund managers. The information that they provide enables the fund manager to make decisions relating to the investment portfolios that they manage.

» **Management consultancy**: advising private and public sector organisations on business issues. Management consultants are primarily concerned with initiating and implementing technological, organisational and behavioural change.

» **Market-research executive**: conducts or commissions market research by planning and controlling projects usually for independent research agencies.

» **Political-party research officer**: responsible for making sure that the party for which they work is able to develop realistic new policies in response to, or in anticipation of, changing social, political and economic conditions.

» **Statistician**: concerned with the collection, analysis, interpretation and presentation of quantitative information. Statisticians design samples, collect data using a variety of methods, process data and advise on the strengths and limitations of results.

» **Trader**: involves undertaking transactions in stocks and shares, bonds, foreign exchange currencies, options or futures with traders at commercial banks, investment banks and large institutional investors.

Further information

The Economist magazine
Dransfield, Robert, *Key Ideas in Economics*, Nelson Thornes 2003
Government Economics Service – www.ges.gov.uk
Institute of Economic Affairs – www.iea.org.uk

Engineering (Applied A level)

One definition of engineering is that it 'involves the knowledge of the mathematical and natural sciences (biological and physical) gained by study, experience and practice that are applied with judgment and creativity to develop ways to utilise the materials and forces of nature for the benefit of mankind'. The A level in this subject introduces students to all areas of engineering and provides some of the skills and knowledge that enable you to work in this sector in the future.

Main elements of the course

This A level is only currently offered by Edexcel and so the outline below is based on this particular syllabus.

» Unit 1: engineering materials, processes and techniques
» Unit 2: the role of the engineer
» Unit 3: principles of design, planning and prototyping
» Unit 4: applied engineering systems
» Unit 5: the engineering environment
» Unit 6: applied design, planning and prototyping.

This course is available in both AS single award (three units) and A level single award (six units).

How is A level Engineering taught and assessed?

Teaching is through a combination of practical project work, case studies, talks from practising engineers and other learning from work-related contexts. Assessment is a mixture of internal and external examination and producing portfolios of evidence. To do well in this subject, students need a practical mind, a head for figures and some lateral thinking skills.

Choosing other A levels to go with Engineering

Other subjects that would go well with Engineering include Mathematics, Physics, Computing, and Design and Technology.

Engineering at higher-education level

There are many different types of engineering and this is reflected in the types of Engineering courses available at degree level. Interestingly, most universities specify A levels in Mathematics and Physics rather than any previous engineering qualifications, so bear this in mind when choosing your subjects.

A degree in Engineering?

Some of the Engineering degrees available include:

- Electronic and Electrical Engineering
- Civil Engineering
- Chemical Engineering
- Mechanical Engineering
- Telecommunications Engineering.

Some of the courses have better links with the engineering industry than others; investigate this before taking the plunge.

Combining Engineering with other degree subjects

Engineering goes well with a number of subjects, most notably Mathematics and Physics. A few combinations currently offered by universities include:

- Engineering with Business Management
- Electronic Engineering with Computer Science
- Engineering with Business Finance
- Civil with Environmental Engineering
- Chemical Engineering with Biochemical Engineering.

Foundation degrees and HNDs

There are many engineering-related Foundation degrees available and you can search for them at www.ucas.com. There are also HNDs available in many different types of engineering and these are listed on the websites of exam boards such as Edexcel.

Engineering and your future career

Non-graduate jobs

With an A level in Engineering, you will be made aware of the career routes open to you in engineering and you may be able to get a place on some training schemes or Apprenticeships with engineering and construction companies. Non-engineering positions will still be open to you, of course.

Graduate jobs related to Engineering
Opportunities in engineering fall into the following categories, but differ in detail and context:

» Engineering research and development
» Engineering design
» Installation and commissioning engineering
» Process engineering, control and maintenance
» Commercial engineering and customer services
» Manufacturing and processing
» Information technology and management services.

Postgraduate qualifications can be valuable if you want to specialise, but further study is essential only if you want to pursue a career in research.

Graduate jobs in which Engineering could be useful
The following represent some of the other potential areas of employment.

» **Chartered management accountant**: provides financial information needed for planning and control of industrial or commercial companies, establishes and maintains financial policies and systems.
» **Management consultant**: provides advice on corporate strategy, organisational development, financial and administrative systems, human resources and information technology.
» **Production manager**: plans, co-ordinates and operates manufacturing and allied production processes to ensure most efficient use of plant, manpower and materials.
» **Systems analyst/systems developer**: investigates and analyses a client's data-processing needs. Designs, tests and implements a system to meet these needs. Writes new programs or modifies existing software to run the system.
» **Technical sales engineer**: acts as a link between a company producing technical goods and services and its customers, negotiating sales, orders, price and quality in order to meet their technical and commercial requirements.

Further information
Association for Women in Science and Engineering – www.awise.org
Construction Careers Website – www.careersinconstruction.com
Institution of Mechanical Engineers – www.imeche.org.uk

English Language

What are the origins of the English language? How has it changed over time? How is it used differently according to different situations, contexts and purposes? What makes the journalism in one newspaper different from another? What is jargon, idiom and cliché? How is language used differently in poetry, drama and prose? Students will consider these kinds of questions as well as developing the skills to critically analyse a piece of writing and learning what makes effective communication in the English language.

Main elements of the course

The outline below is based on what the majority of exam-board syllabuses include. For an exact definition of the syllabus you will be studying, you should consult your school or college or even the exam board itself. Students who are finding it difficult to choose between English Language and English Literature should be aware that OCR offers a combined course in English Language and Literature, but your school or college might not be able to offer this option. AEA level in English is available to students of the course. It is offered through OCR exam board.

Introduction to language study

Students explore a variety of texts to learn some of the characteristics of the English language including structure, stylistics, semantics and linguistics.

Using language

This element of the course allows students to develop their own writing skills and compare what they have written to a series of texts.

Interacting through language
Students study how language is used in face-to-face encounters and identify the speaking and listening skills required to be an effective communicator. Includes theorists' views of face-to-face communication and linguistic analysis.

Language variation and change
How language is used in different times and settings is the focus of this part of the course and students learn how the language has developed since the sixteenth century to the present day. Students are also taught how contemporary English is used differently in different geographical locations.

How is A level English Language taught and assessed?

As well as receiving teacher-led input, students will analyse texts from the present day and the past. To do well in this subject students should enjoy both reading and writing and possess a curiosity about the English language. AS candidates do half of the A2 course and both elements are examined by written exams and independent coursework.

Choosing other A level subjects to go with English Language

Good complements to this subject include English Literature, History, Latin and Greek, and Media and Communication Studies, but it can be combined with almost any A level.

English Language at higher-education level

There are many variations of English Language degrees at university level. Some are combined with English Literature; others are called Language and Linguistic Science. Choose your institution carefully, depending on the kind of course you want. Some institutions, but by no means all, may stipulate English Language A level, and some may require at least a GCSE in a foreign language.

A degree in English Language?

The kinds of things you could study in an English Language and Linguistics degree might include:

- Phonetics (physical nature of speech)
- Phonology (use of sounds in language)
- Morphology (word formation)
- Syntax (sentence structure)

- » Semantics (meaning of words and how they combine into sentences)
- » Pragmatics (effect of situation on language use)
- » Theoretical linguistics (pure and simple: how languages work)
- » Historical linguistics (how languages got to be the way they are)
- » Sociolinguistics (language and the structure of society).

Combining English Language with other degree subjects

As well as Linguistics, this subject is often combined with a modern foreign language, Literature, Music, Anthropology, Classics and Philosophy. In theory, it could be combined with any other subject, but combinations often depend upon the willingness of the academic departments involved.

Foundation degrees and HNDs

There aren't currently any Foundation degrees in English Language but there are a few courses related to Literature and Cultural Studies that could be of interest to some students. There is no HND in this subject.

English Language and your future career

Non-graduate jobs

All employers want people who can communicate well and this subject certainly enables students to develop their communication skills. Jobs in customer service, administration, marketing and sales all require these skills.

Graduate jobs related to English (Language)

If you wish to use your degree directly there are several employment areas where a degree in English is directly relevant. Some of the most popular jobs are listed below. Further study is needed in some cases.

- » **Higher-education lecturer in English language**: teaching university students about language and linguistics. After your first degree, you would generally need an MA and a PhD to get a lectureship.
- » **Primary/secondary-school teacher**: opportunities exist in secondary and primary schools as well as in independent schools, sixth-form colleges and in further or higher education.
- » **Teacher of English as a foreign/second language**: teaching English to foreign students either in the UK or overseas.

Graduate jobs in which a degree in English (Language) would be useful

There are careers which traditionally attract English graduates more than others and which can make use of many of the skills that are acquired through studying the subject.

- **Advertising account executive**: co-ordinates, plans and organises advertising campaigns in consultation with clients.
- **Advertising copywriter**: writes original advertising copy to promote and sell products or services in the press, on television and radio or on posters.
- **Arts administrator**: works in theatres, arts centres, arts and heritage organisations to ensure that the artistic programme actually happens. Includes organising, planning, marketing and financial aspects.
- **Charity officer**: involves a wide range of responsibilities including aspects of marketing, finance, fund-raising, public relations etc. Includes organising events, managing volunteers, meeting targets, etc.
- **Commissioning editor**: monitors the progress from commissioning to production and liaises with people involved with production of material. Develops ideas and responds to market forces.
- **Marketing executive**: formulates a marketing plan for a product/service and brings it to fruition.
- **Newspaper journalist**: reports on news and other items of current interest for newspapers.
- **Public-relations officer**: projects and maintains a desirable image of an organisation and keeps the public informed of developments of general interest.
- **Television/film/video producer**: responsible for turning ideas into programmes within the allocated budget.
- **Television programme researcher**: generates programme ideas, researches background material, briefs production teams and presenters.

Further information

Bryson, Bill, *Mother Tongue*, Penguin, 1991
Gardiner, Alan, *English Language: A level Study Guide*, Longman, 2003
Society of Authors – www.societyofauthors.net

English Language and Literature

The GCE A/AS level in English Language and Literature allows students the opportunity to study English from both a linguistic and a literary perspective. It gives them the opportunity to study a far more varied range of texts than for a pure literature course and is less focused on structure, semantics and linguistics than a pure language course. Some of the questions that students of this course consider include:

» How do language and literature link together?
» How is language used in particular literary genres such as poetry, prose and drama?
» How do I critically compare two or more pieces of literature and/or language?
» How is language adapted according to different audiences?

Main elements of the course
The outline below is based on what the majority of exam-board syllabuses include. For an exact definition of the AS and A2 syllabus you will be studying, you should consult your school or college or even the exam board itself. AEA level in English is available to students of the course. It is offered through OCR exam board.

Linking language and literature
This unit requires students to compare literary texts with a piece of non-literary language such as a transcript of speech. In this way, students learn how different meanings are created by different literary and linguistic forms.

Language in literature: poetry and prose
Students study various texts of poetry and prose, usually in preparation for a final examination where they have to give a close textual comment, using both literary and linguistic analysis. The syllabus currently includes texts by Robert Frost, Chaucer, Emily Brontë, Wendy Cope, Philip Larkin and Ian McEwan.

Styles of writing
In this module students write original pieces covering both literary and non-literary styles and also provide a commentary on their own writing based on the insights gained from both literary and linguistic techniques.

Language in literature: drama
Different dramatic texts are studied, usually including both Shakespeare and more contemporary plays. In the exam, students have to comment on a particular passage of text and relate it to the whole piece from both a literary and linguistic perspective. Texts currently on offer include: *The Tempest, As You Like it, Hamlet, King Lear, Waiting for Godot* and *A Streetcar Named Desire*.

Issues in language and literature
Focuses on how language and literature can be used and interpreted according to different social and political agendas. For the OCR syllabus, for instance, students can choose to focus on the 'language of persuasion', 'language and identities' and 'language and gender'.

Genre studies
Most syllabuses have a synoptic module where students link together all they have learned on the course so far and, during an examination, are required to answer questions on unseen pieces of text and/or literature.

How is English Language and Literature taught and assessed?
As with the study of pure literature and pure language, teaching is a combination of close textual analysis in classes and group discussions about particular themes. Students are also expected to do plenty of reading outside the classroom to support their learning. There will be lots of essay writing throughout the course. Assessment is via a combination of coursework, closed examinations and 'open book' examinations. As with many other subjects, the AS can be taken as a stand-alone subject or taken as 50% of the assessment value towards the final A2 mark.

Choosing other A level subjects to go with English Language and Literature

It is common to see students combine this A level with other arts and humanities subjects such as History, a foreign language or Geography. Certainly the kind of skills used in these A levels would reinforce and complement the ones developed in the study of language and literature. However, this subject would also provide a good contrast for students who are opting to study more science-based subjects for their other A levels.

English Language and Literature at higher-education level

At degree level, there are many courses that include language and literature. Sometimes this degree is offered jointly by the departments of Literature and Linguistics. To get a place on one of these degree courses you would need a good A level grade in at least one of the following: English Language and Literature, English Literature or English Language.

A degree in English Language and Literature?

As with most degrees, there are usually some core modules, and then students can opt to specialise in certain areas should they choose. Current degrees in this subject include modules such as 'The English Language', 'Old English', 'English Literature: 1740–1842', 'Reading Literature', 'Language Studies' and many others. Some degree courses have a foreign language and literature element so having an A level in a foreign language could be a help to study this subject at degree level.

Combining English Language and Literature with other degree subjects

Given that English Language and Literature is already a combined degree of sorts, it's not that common to see it combined further with other subjects. However, as mentioned above, the study of a foreign language or literature, or a more in-depth study of linguistics, is often involved.

Foundation Degrees and HNDs

HNDs and Foundation Degrees in English Language and Literature are still uncommon. They do exist, however, in related areas and in vocational areas where the knowledge and study of English is useful, such as media and communications, journalism, advertising, publishing and business with English as a foreign language.

English Language and Literature and your future career

Non-graduate jobs

Many employers requiring A levels do not really mind which subjects applicants have. In that sense, English Language and Literature A level is as good a choice as any. However, there may be some non-graduate areas of work where English Language and Literature A level is still more useful than some others because you will have developed strong skills in both written and oral communication. Jobs where these skills are especially useful include:

» Marketing or sales assistants
» Jobs requiring a lot of communication or telephone work
» Trainee news reporter
» Library assistant
» Tour guide.

Graduate jobs directly related to English Language or Literature

If you wish to use your degree directly there are several employment areas where a degree in English is directly relevant. Some of the most popular jobs are listed below. Further training is needed in some cases.

» **Higher-education lecturer in English Language and Literature**: teaching university students about language or literature. After your degree, you would generally need an MA and a PhD to get a lectureship.
» **Primary/secondary-school teacher**: opportunities exist in secondary and primary schools as well as in independent schools, sixth-form colleges and in further or higher education.
» **Teacher of English as a foreign/second language**: teaching English to foreign students in either the UK or overseas.

Graduate jobs where English Language and Literature would be useful

There are careers which traditionally attract English graduates more than others and which can make use of many of the skills that are acquired through studying the subject.

» **Advertising account executive**: co-ordinates, plans and organises advertising campaigns in consultation with clients.
» **Advertising copywriter**: writes original advertising copy to promote and sell products or services in the press, on television and radio or on posters.

- **Arts administrator**: works in theatres, arts centres, arts and heritage organisations to ensure that the artistic programme actually happens. Includes organising, planning, marketing and financial aspects.
- **Charity officer**: involves a wide range of responsibilities including aspects of marketing, finance, fund-raising, public relations, etc. Includes organising events, managing volunteers, meeting targets etc.
- **Commissioning editor**: monitors the progress from commissioning to production and liaises with people involved with production of material. Develops ideas and responds to market forces.
- **Marketing executive**: formulates a marketing plan for a product/service and brings it to fruition.
- **Newspaper journalist**: reports on news and other items of current interest for newspapers.
- **Public-relations officer**: projects and maintains a desirable image of an organisation and keeps the public informed of developments of general interest.
- **Television/film/video producer**: responsible for turning ideas into programmes within the allocated budget.
- **Television programme researcher**: generates programme ideas, researches background material, briefs production teams and presenters.

Further information

Baldick, Chris, *Concise Dictionary of Literary Terms*, OUP, 2004
Bryson, Bill, *Mother Tongue*, Penguin, 1991
Gardiner, Alan, *English Language and Literature: A level Revise Guide*, Pearson Education, 2005
National Council for the Training of Journalists – www.nctj.com
Society of Authors – www.societyofauthors.net

English Literature

A level English Literature involves the study of texts and their meaning in many different contexts: critical, historical, social, psychological and so on. Through the appreciation of literature, students are asked to think about a whole range of questions about life. Literature intersects with many other subjects such as History, Psychology, Philosophy, Religion, Art and Sociology. The kinds of issues A level English Literature students could consider include:

» What is the author's view of contemporary society?
» What literary methods does the poet use to create a particular effect in the poem?
» How does Shakespeare's language differ from our own?
» What are the main recurring themes in this novel?

Students generally have the opportunity to get to grips with a selection of drama, poetry and fiction. Usually there are certain 'set texts' from which the school may choose for the AS and A2 qualification and these will vary from exam board to exam board. It is very common, however, for there to be some study of Shakespeare.

Main elements of the course
The outline below is based on what the majority of exam-board syllabuses include. For an exact definition of the AS and A2 syllabus you will be studying, you should consult your school or college or even the exam board itself, especially as set texts will vary. Students who are finding it difficult to choose between English Language and English Literature should be aware that OCR offers a combined course in English Language and Literature, but your school or college might not be able to offer this

option. AEA level in English is available to students of the course. It is offered through OCR exam board.

Drama
Students are usually required to study drama and a Shakespeare play is often one of their set texts. These also vary from year to year but common choices by exam boards include *Henry IV Part 1*, *Henry IV Part 2*, *King Lear*, *As You Like It*, *Othello* and *Macbeth*.

Prose/fiction
Most syllabuses also include a stipulation that students gain a knowledge of modern and older fiction. Some exam boards make the distinction between pre- and post-war writing (ie before and after 1914). Popular texts for study include: Charlotte Brontë's *Jane Eyre*; Bram Stoker's *Dracula*; Harper Lee's *To Kill a Mockingbird*; John Steinbeck's *Of Mice and Men*; Thomas Hardy's *Tess of the D'Urbervilles*; Joseph Conrad's *Heart of Darkness* and many others.

Poetry
English has a rich history of poetry, therefore exam boards have a lot to choose from. Again, choices reflect both modern and older poets and set texts can include some of Chaucer's *Canterbury Tales* and Shakespeare's sonnets, and selected poems from the following writers:

» Sylvia Plath
» Seamus Heaney
» T S Eliot
» Tony Harris
» Anne Stevenson
» William Blake
» John Keats
» W B Yeats
» Tony Harrison.

How is English Literature taught and assessed?
As you would expect, there is a lot of independent reading involved in the study of literature. Classes involve going through some of the set texts in detail, but supporting reading is often required outside the classroom. English Literature is a demanding subject in terms of both the volume of reading and the volume of essay writing. Students are sometimes encouraged to enact a section of a play they are studying: this often helps bring alive the text. Students should also take advantage of going to the theatre to see the play they are studying being performed, if this is at all possible. Like many other subjects, English Literature A level is

assessed using a combination of coursework and written examinations. Again, as with many other subjects, the AS can be taken as a stand-alone subject or as 50% of the assessment value towards the final A2 mark.

Choosing other A level subjects to go with English Literature

It's common to see students combine this A level with other arts and humanities subjects such as History, a foreign language or Geography. Certainly, the kind of skills used in these A levels would reinforce and complement the ones developed in the study of literature.

English Literature at higher-education level

At degree level, English Literature is a very popular subject indeed. There are many different variations and combinations of the subject at this level, such as English and Related Literature (which includes the study of some foreign literature), English Language and Literature, and English Literature and Society. Most of these would require a good A level grade in English Literature, although some institutions may accept you onto a course if you have an A level in English Language.

A degree in English Literature?

At most institutions, there will be some core components to a course (such as Medieval English, Shakespeare or the Victorian Period) and lots of different modules or 'special papers' from which students can choose, such as James Joyce, Modern American Poetry, Chaucer, Post-Colonial Writing and so on. Many degree courses have a foreign language and literature element, so an A level in a foreign language could be a help with studying literature at degree level.

Combining English Literature with other degree subjects

Given that the study of literature overlaps with so many other subjects, it's fairly common for students to combine it with other subjects. The following combinations are especially common:

» English and History
» English and Philosophy
» English and French Literature
» English and Sociology
» English and Media Studies
» English and Politics.

Foundation degrees and HNDs

HNDs and Foundation degrees in English Literature are still pretty uncommon. They do exist, however, in related areas and in vocational areas where the knowledge and study of English is useful, such as media and communications, journalism, advertising and publishing.

English Literature and your future career

Non-graduate jobs

Many employers requiring A levels do not really mind which subjects applicants have, so English Literature A level is as good a choice as any. However, there may be some non-graduate areas of work where English Literature A level is still more useful than others because you will have developed strong skills in both written and oral communication. Jobs where these skills are especially useful include:

- Marketing or sales assistants
- Jobs requiring a lot of communication or telephone work
- Trainee news reporter
- Library assistant
- Tour guide.

Graduate jobs directly related to English or English Literature

If you wish to use your degree directly there are several employment areas in which a degree in English is directly relevant. Some of the most popular jobs are listed below. Further training is needed in some cases.

- **Higher-education lecturer in English language**: teaching university students about language and linguistics. After your first degree, you would generally need an MA and a PhD to get a lectureship.
- **Primary/secondary-school teacher**: opportunities exist in secondary and primary schools as well as in independent schools, sixth-form colleges and in further or higher education.
- **Teacher of English as a foreign/second language**: teaching English to foreign students either in the UK or overseas.

Graduate jobs in which English or English Literature would be useful

There are careers which traditionally attract English graduates more than others and which can make use of many of the skills that are acquired through studying the subject.

» **Advertising account executive**: co-ordinates, plans and organises advertising campaigns in consultation with clients.
» **Advertising copywriter**: writes original advertising copy to promote and sell products or services in the press, on television and radio or on posters.
» **Arts administrator**: works in theatres, arts centres, arts and heritage organisations to ensure that the artistic programme actually happens. Includes organising, planning, marketing and financial aspects.
» **Charity officer**: involves a wide range of responsibilities including aspects of marketing, finance, fund-raising, public relations, etc. Includes organising events, managing volunteers, meeting targets, etc.
» **Commissioning editor**: monitors the progress from commissioning to production and liaises with people involved with production of material. Develops ideas and responds to market forces.
» **Marketing executive**: formulates a marketing plan for a product/service and brings it to fruition.
» **Newspaper journalist**: reports on news and other items of current interest for newspapers.
» **Public-relations officer**: projects and maintains a desirable image of an organisation and keeps the public informed of developments of general interest.
» **Television/film/video producer**: responsible for turning ideas into programmes within the allocated budget.
» **Television programme researcher**: generates programme ideas, researches background material, briefs production teams and presenters.

Further information

Baldick, Chris, *Concise Dictionary of Literary Terms*, OUP
National Council for the Training of Journalists – www.nctj.com
Society of Authors – www.societyofauthors.net

Environmental Science

Environmental Science is all about how humans interact with their environment. Given the growing public and political concern about environmental issues, it is hardly a surprise that this subject is becoming more and more popular among A level students. Students learn about the scientific concepts in relation to environmentalism, but also the social, political and economic aspects of managing the environment.

Main elements of the course

The outline below is based on what the majority of exam-board syllabuses include. For an exact definition of the syllabus you will be studying, you should consult your school or college or even the exam board itself. The requirements of A2 and AS Environmental Science are different: the AS focuses only on the scientific processes that take place in the environment whereas A2 level also covers environmental management.

Energy, atmosphere and hydrosphere

This unit looks at solar radiation and energy transfer – the effect of human actions on the climate and atmosphere (eg acid rain, the ozone layer and global warming). It also introduces students to how water moves around in the atmosphere.

The lithosphere

Minerals, rocks and soil on and below the earth's surface.

The biosphere

This module examines the conditions on Earth that allow organisms to exist and explores ecosystems, energy capture and transfer and populations of living things.

Biotic resource management
This aspect of the course focuses on how humans use the environment and its resources in order to survive. Topics such as crop production, agricultural systems, deforestation and genetic engineering as well as their social and environmental impacts are all explored.

Pollution and physical resource management
This unit explores issues such as: the properties of pollutants; waste disposal; water conservation and pollution; air pollution; noise pollution and radiation.

How is A level Environmental Science taught and assessed?

As well as taking part in teacher-led activities, students will examine case studies of environmental issues, work on scenario planning, conduct cost-benefit analyses and energy audits, and much more. Assessment is via a combination of assessed practical work and written exams occurring at different points in the course and depending on whether you are an A2 or AS candidate.

Choosing other A level subjects to go with Environmental Science

Environmental Science obviously goes very well with Geography and Biology, but other subjects that are compatible include Politics, Economics and Law. Most degree courses won't specify that an A level in Environmental Science is needed, but most prefer at least A level Geography.

Environmental Science at higher-education level

Environmental Science at higher-education level is often taught by Geography departments and it may be called Environmental Studies or Environmental Policy rather than Environmental Science. Most degrees emphasise the importance of integrating Biology, Chemistry and Geography in order to understand the science of human impact on the environment, and how these need to be applied within the context of social, legal and political frameworks to resolve some of the major environmental issues facing the world.

A degree in Environmental Science?

A typical degree in this subject would have some core subjects in the first year with some options in the second and third years. Instruction takes the form of lectures, tutorials, seminars, practicals, fieldwork and research projects, all of which vary in form and content between departments. Fieldwork includes specific field-project modules as well as projects on air and water quality. Most students are required to undertake final-year research projects and these may also include a substantial element of fieldwork.

Combining Environmental Science with other degree subjects

It is quite common to see this subject combined with Physics, Biology, Chemistry, Mathematics, Geography, Politics and Computer Science.

Foundation degrees and HNDs

There are a number of Environmental Science-related Foundation degrees, which you can search for at www.ucas.com, and Edexcel offers an HND in Environmental Science.

Environmental Science and your future career

Non-graduate jobs

Most jobs in the Environmental Science field involve further training, but you may be able to get some experience in environmental charities, especially if you have good administrative or secretarial skills. Your A level in this subject will have developed your skills in analysis, logical thinking and problem solving and you should always try to demonstrate these to potential employers, whatever the sector.

Graduate jobs related to Environmental Science

There has been an increase in the range of careers for which an Environmental Science degree is required. Postgraduate qualifications may be necessary or desirable. Some jobs related to Environmental Science include:

- **Countryside manager**: works for a local authority to manage countryside and visitor services within that area.
- **Environmental education officer**: supports, sustains and develops environmental issues within the community. May involve school visits, giving talks, leading walks, producing educational resources and developing innovative ways of promoting sustainable development.
- **Environmental manager**: implements initiatives through local authorities in the UK, eg sustainable development programmes,

programmes for the reduction of pollution and other environmentally linked policies in their area.

» **Nature conservation officer**: responsible for the protection, management and development of wildlife habitats in a National or Country Park, private estate or other conservation site.

» **Recycling officer**: responsible for local authorities' environmental policies for waste reduction, re-use and recovery. Develops plans, implements and monitors a variety of recycling schemes.

» **Waste-disposal officer**: works with local authorities, which are responsible for waste regulation, or with waste-disposal companies in the fields of: site operations; control and monitoring of the environmental effects of waste disposal; developing new methods of managing all types of waste disposal (recycling, high-temperature incineration, etc).

» **Water-quality scientist**: scientific analysis of water samples to maintain quality and to set targets and standards.

Graduate jobs in which a degree in Environmental Science could be useful

» **Environmental consultant**: works on client contracts in areas such as water pollution, air and land contamination, waste management, environmental impact assessment, environmental audit, ecological management, environmental policy, etc.

» **Environmental-health officer**: monitors and ensures the maintenance of standards of environmental and public health – including food and food hygiene, safety at work, housing, noise and pollution control – in accordance with the law.

» **Property and construction**: landscape architecture, town planning, cartography, geographical information systems.

» **Public health and consumer protection**: occupational and public health, health and safety inspectorates, environmental health.

» **Secondary-school teacher**: Geography or Science, depending on core subjects in first degree.

» **Toxicologist**: carries out scientific identification and studies effects of harmful chemicals, biological materials and radiation on living systems and the environment to see how they can be avoided or minimised.

» **Transportation planner**: identifies need for transport infrastructure, manages travel demand and changes people's travel behaviour in line with government guidelines, eg reducing car use and promoting walking, cycling and public transport.

Further information

Byrne, Kevin, *Environmental Science*, Nelson Byrnes
Department for Environment, Food and Rural Affairs (DEFRA) –
www.defra.gov.uk
Environment Agency – www.environment-agency.gov.uk

Film Studies

As a student of A level Film Studies you will broaden and deepen both your knowledge and enjoyment of films. The emphasis of the course is on how films convey meanings in different ways and how they are subject to the social, cultural, political and economic forces of the time at which they were created. As well as analysing different genres of film, students will compare Hollywood and British films and analyse specific cinematic techniques. How the film and cinema industry operates is also part of this course.

Main elements of the course

At the time of writing, the only exam board to offer this course is WJEC, so the following outline is based on its specification.

Unit 1: film – making meaning 1

This unit focuses on analysing the form and style of certain types of film, usually but not necessarily Hollywood films. The relationship between form and how an audience interprets a film is also an important part of this.

Unit 2: producers and audiences (Hollywood and British cinema)

This module addresses the social practice of film watching and cinema-going, as well as the economic and social aspects of the film industry.

Unit 3: messages and values (British and Irish cinema)

This unit focuses on how messages, meanings and values are conveyed in filmic representation, with particular emphasis on British and Irish cinema.

Unit 4: film – making meaning 2
Students have to carry out research focusing on the relationship between meaning and production and produce some creative work themselves.

Unit 5: studies in world cinema
Students learn about the different cinema content and styles from around the world and compare and contrast them.

Unit 6: critical studies
This is a synoptic module, bringing together the learning from all the different units and addressing cinematic themes which intersect them, eg documentary, experimental film making, shocking cinema, etc.

Students who want to complete the AS qualification complete only the first three units; A2 students need to complete all six.

How is A level Film Studies taught and assessed?
Obviously there will be a lot of time spent watching films, although this will probably be in your own time. Classes will involve discussions, looking at clips and critical comparisons of different films. Assessment is by a combination of internally assessed coursework and written examinations marked by the exam board.

Choosing other A level subjects to go with Film Studies
Subjects that complement this one include Media Studies, English Literature, Communication Studies, a modern foreign language, Sociology and History. Always ensure that there isn't too much of an overlap between your subjects because exam boards may not permit the combination and universities may not recognise your UCAS points tally.

Film Studies at higher-education level
There are many film courses at higher-education level. Some are very academic or theoretical, others are more practical or vocational in their approach. You have to decide which type of course appeals to you more. There are also many related courses in Media Studies or Media Arts, and studying film would constitute a large part of that.

A degree in Film Studies?
The breadth of your studies will be much greater at degree level than at A level. Usually there are some core modules in the first year with some flexibility of choice of modules in years two and three. Some typical modules of a degree in Film Studies might include:

- Introduction to narrative cinema
- Art and film
- Avant garde cinema
- Cinema in 1920s Berlin, Paris and Moscow
- The documentary film
- European cinema
- Sound and cinema
- Border crossings in American cinema
- British cinema from the 1950s
- Film style, interpretation and evaluation
- Topics in American cinema.

Combining Film Studies with other degree subjects

Subjects that are often combined with Film Studies include: English Literature, a modern language, Contemporary Arts, Drama, History and Politics.

Foundation degrees and HNDs

There are Foundation degrees available in Film and Television Production and also specific areas of media, but none specifically in Film Studies alone. You can search for them at www.ucas.com. There are also a number of HNDs in media-related subjects.

Film Studies and your future career

Non-graduate jobs

An A level in Film Studies will give you good skills and an insight into the film industry as well as the academic aspects of film. Getting into the film business as a career is notoriously difficult and you have to be prepared to make contacts and often work without pay to build experience until you get your first break. Non-media careers are still open to you, of course.

Graduate jobs related to Film Studies

Many students on these courses are interested in gaining employment in all aspects of the media industry. Careers in the media, however, are highly sought after and competition is likely to be fierce.

- **Broadcast assistant, radio**: assists with production and presentation of programmes for local and national radio stations.
- **Broadcasting presenter**: fronts the programme; specific responsibilities vary depending on the programme.
- **Journalism**: reports on news and other areas of interest for newspapers, periodicals, radio and TV.

» **Multimedia programmer**: researches, develops and produces materials for new-media-based company activities.
» **Programme researcher, broadcasting/film/video**: acts as an assistant producer with responsibility for conception and implementation of a programme.
» **Radio producer**: responsible for initiating ideas, selling these to commissioning editors and managing the technical and creative team to produce the final programme.
» **Television/film/video producer**: undertakes the artistic interpretation of materials and directs the production of shows/films.
» **Television production assistant**: provides organisational and secretarial services for programme director.

Graduate jobs in which a degree in Film Studies could be useful

» **Advertising account executive**: takes overall responsibility for co-ordinating, planning and organising advertising campaigns.
» **Information officer/manager**: ensures effective communication of information relating to a particular field of interest.
» **Event organiser**: identifies potential business, researches, writes, plans and runs all types of conference on behalf of a client or his/her own organisation.
» **Market-research executive**: undertakes systematic research to determine the potential market for a product or service.
» **Public-relations account executive**: PR agencies work for their clients in presenting their image to the public. They decide on strategies to be used and which media would be the most effective.

Further information
British Film Institute – www.bfi.org.uk/education
Skillset – www.skillset.org; www.skillsformedia.com
O'Sullivan, Tim *et al, Studying the Media*, Hodder Arnold, 1998

General Studies

General Studies is a bit different from most A level subjects in that it is not the study of a single discipline; instead, it seeks to broaden students' minds by teaching aspects of various different disciplines and areas of life. As well as learning about issues and acquiring knowledge of contemporary and historical matters, one of the aims of the course is to develop in students the skills of critical and logical thinking so that they can form their own opinions.

Main elements of the course

The outline below is based on what the majority of exam-board syllabuses include, but there is often some variation in the title of modules. For an exact definition of the syllabus you will be studying, you should consult your school or college or even the exam board itself. Some of the themes studied include:

» Culture, morality, arts and humanities
» Science, mathematics and technology
» Society, politics and the economy
» Critical thinking and analytical skills.

How is A level General Studies taught and assessed?

A level candidates usually have about four compulsory units plus two optional ones, AS candidates usually have two compulsory options and one optional module. Assessment is via a combination of written exams and coursework. You don't need GCSE General Studies to study this subject. In fact, some schools and colleges make A level General Studies a compulsory part of their A level programme.

Choosing other subjects to go with A level General Studies

Some universities do not recognise General Studies as a qualifying subject – General Studies should be taken in addition to your 'regular' subjects, not instead of them. In this sense any other subjects may be added to the General Studies course.

General Studies at higher-education level

There are no degree programmes in General Studies.

Foundation degrees and HNDs

There are no Foundation degrees or HNDs in this subject.

General Studies and your future career

There are no specific jobs related to this subject, but employers appreciate people who have a broad knowledge base and who can think for themselves. General Studies aims to equip students with both of these things. However, like many universities, many employers don't recognise General Studies as a 'legitimate' A level subject.

Geography

Students of Geography learn about the environment in which we live and the way humans interact with and in that environment. On the one hand students learn about the physical aspects of the earth (physical geography) and on the other they learn about how humans use and adapt to their surroundings (human/urban geography) as well as the interaction between the two. Geography is a truly interdisciplinary subject, calling on and developing skills in research, numeracy and spatial awareness, as well as critical and analytical thinking. Some of the most basic political issues are often considered by A level geographers, including: decisions to build new motorways or runways; the effects of natural disasters and floods; immigration; food shortage and famine.

Main elements of the course

For an exact definition of the AS and A2 syllabus you will be studying, you should consult your school, college or the exam board itself. AS candidates do a proportion of the total A2 course, taking the core units plus an element of 'Geographical Skills'. This subject is also offered at AEA level by WJEC exam board.

Core concepts in physical geography

- » Water on land
- » Climatic hazards and change
- » Energy and life.

Core concepts in human geography

- » Population dynamics
- » Settlement processes and patterns
- » Economic activity.

Challenge and change in the natural environment

» Coasts – processes and problems
» Geomorphological processes and hazards (the shaping of the earth's surfaces by environmental forces)
» Cold environments and human activity.

How is A level Geography taught and assessed?

Like most subjects there is an element of learning from text books and classroom note-taking. However, students of this subjects will work with maps, statistical data, weather reports and case studies; they will carry out surveys, create questionnaires and watch videos. They will also carry out fieldwork and may visit locations of geographical interest. To do well at this subject, students need to be good all-rounders with the ability to think about and analyse different types of data.

Most exam boards offer two different types of Geography A level syllabus. Depending on the syllabus chosen by the school or college, it may not be necessary to have studied GCSE Geography to study it at A level.

Choosing other A level subjects to go with Geography

Geography can be very scientific at one end of the spectrum and very social at the other. In this sense, it can go very well with a wide range of subjects. Common accompaniments to the subject include Environmental Science, Biology, History, Mathematics, Physics and Chemistry. If you want to study Geography at higher-education level, then it could affect your choice of A levels because some degree courses are very science based while others are much more humanities based.

Geography at higher-education level

Geography at degree level can be offered as a science subject (BSc) or an arts subject (BA) or both. This largely depends on the outlook of the department and the emphasis of a particular course. Most institutions will want you to have A level Geography, but there may be some exceptions.

A degree in Geography?

A Geography BSc tends to focus more on physical geography and the Geography BA tends to focus more on human geography. Some universities offer some flexibility so that students can choose options from both degree programmes. Despite this, there are usually some core courses (usually in the first year at least) and thereafter some choice about the remaining modules to be taken. Fieldwork is also an important part of a degree in Geography and many institutions run fieldwork trips in

Britain and abroad. Some of the modules that could form part of a typical degree programme in Geography include the following:

- Geography, society and development
- Global environmental issues
- Methods in geographical analysis
- The natural environment
- Readings in geography
- Global environmental change
- Historical geographies of urbanism
- Hydrology
- Natural hazards
- Global environmental problems and policies
- Tropical forests in a changing environment.

Combining Geography with other degree subjects

If allowed by the institution, Geography can be combined with many other degree subjects including a modern foreign language, Environmental Science, History, Computer Science, Development Studies, English and Biology.

Foundation degrees and HNDs

There are no Foundation degrees specifically in Geography but there are some in environment-related topics. Similarly, there are no HNDs in Geography but there are some in the area of land and environmental studies.

Geography and your future career

Non-graduate jobs

You will gain lots of varied skills from A level Geography that you could apply to many different areas of work. If you want to work in a geography-related area, though, you would probably have to study the subject at degree level first.

Graduate jobs related to Geography

Some of the following jobs require further training or study and relevant practical experience.

- **Cartographer**: evaluates sets of geographical data and presents it in the form of diagrams, charts and spreadsheets as well as conventional maps.
- **Distribution/logistics manager**: manages the supply, movement and storage of goods and materials. You would plan, organise and co-

ordinate the flow and storage of materials through the whole supply-chain process from manufacturer to customer.

» **Environmental consultant**: works in areas such as air and land contamination, water pollution, noise and vibration measurement, waste management, environmental policy and ecological/land management.

» **Geographical information systems manager**: manages a team of ICT professionals who use computer-based systems to handle geographical information.

» **Remote-sensing scientist**: processes aerial photographs and satellite images by computer in order to fit them to maps or to enhance specific features of interest and to assess their significance.

» **Secondary-school teacher**: develops schemes of work and plans lessons in line with national objectives. As a secondary-school teacher you must also keep up to date with developments in your subject area and with new resources and methods.

» **Town planner**: directs or undertakes the planning of land use. This involves taking into account the views of interested parties in order to find a balance between the conflicting demands of housing, industrial development, agriculture, recreation, transport network, the environment, etc.

» **Transportation planner**: identifies the need for a transport infrastructure, devises transport strategies in line with government guidelines, eg reducing car use and promoting walking, cycling and public transport. Statistical analysis is used to forecast developments.

Graduate jobs in which a degree in Geography could be useful

The following represent some common areas of employment for geographers.

» **Local government administrator**: responds to the needs of individual departments, sometimes as a specialist in administration, finance or personnel. You would assist in the formulation of policies and procedures and co-ordinate their implementation.

» **Nature-conservation officer**: protects, manages and enhances wildlife habitats. Your work may include promoting and implementing local biodiversity action plans through negotiation with planners and developers, conservation tasks, visitor liaison or educational and interpretative work.

» **Tourism officer**: develops and promotes tourism in order to attract visitors and to produce significant economic benefits for a particular region or site.

» **Urban general-practice surveyor**: values, manages and markets residential and commercial property and acts as an agent for clients in the purchase, leasing or sale of property.

Further information

Association of Geographic Information – www.agi.org.uk

Nagle, G, *Advanced Geography*, OUP

Royal Geographical Society – www.rgs.org

Geology

Students of Geology learn about the characteristics of the earth's surface including rocks and soil as well as the rocks and minerals that make up the earth's crust, mantle and core. Geology also gives an insight into the origins of the planet and how it has changed over time. It is also an important discipline because it teaches us much about the causes of natural disasters such as volcanoes, earthquakes and tsunamis.

Main elements of the course
The outline below is based on the OCR exam board, which is one of two exam boards that offers A level Geology, the other being WJEC.

Global tectonics and geological structures
The structure of the earth; earthquakes; global tectonics; geological structures.

The rock cycle – processes and products
The rock cycle (the study of igneous, sedimentary and metamorphic rocks); sedimentary processes and products; igneous processes and products; metamorphic processes and products.

Economic and environmental geology
Water supply; energy resources; metal deposits; applied geology.

Palaeontology (the study of fossils)
Preservation of fossils; morphology; evolution and extinction; palaeoenvironments' mode of life; geological dating.

Petrology (the study of types of rock and stone)
Igneous classification and processes; sedimentary classification and processes; metamorphic classification and processes.

Geological skills
A synoptic module developing observational and interpretive geological skills. Students will have to use the knowledge they have gained from all the different modules to answer the questions on the exam paper.

Students following the AS course study the first three of these modules. A2 candidates study all six.

How is A level Geology taught and assessed?
Geology is a science subject, so practical and lab work is an important element. It is suitable for candidates looking for a broad base in science at A level and also supports subjects such as Geography – the ideas extend GCSE Science and are complementary to AS/Advanced GCE Geography. No previous knowledge of geology is required, but science should have been studied to Intermediate level. Assessment is by written exams, fieldwork and coursework.

Choosing other A level subjects to go with Geology
Other subjects that would go well with Geology at AS or Advanced GCE are Biology, Chemistry, Geography and Physics. Candidates concentrating on arts, humanities or modern-language subjects may wish to take Geology to AS level to broaden their studies by continuing to take a science subject.

Geology at higher-education level
If you want to study Geology at a higher level you will probably need at least two A levels from the following subjects: Physics, Chemistry, Biology, Geology, Geography and Environmental Science.

A degree in Geology?
Some of the Geology-related degree programmes on offer include:

» Geology
» Geophysics
» Geology and Geophysics
» Environmental Geoscience
» Computational Geoscience.

Combining Geology with other degree subjects

Subjects that go well with Geology include: Physics, Biology, Computer Science, Geography, Archaeology and Environmental Science. There will be variations in which combinations universities are prepared to offer.

Foundation degrees and HNDs

There are no Foundation degrees available in Geology but there are HNDs available in Environmental Science, which has some overlap with Geology.

Geology and your future career

Non-graduate jobs

You will gain lots of varied skills from A level Geology that you could apply to many different areas of work. These skills include numeracy, analytical ability, good judgement and ICT skills. If you want to work in a Geology-related area, though, you would probably have to study the subject at a degree level first.

Graduate jobs related to Geology

» **Engineering geologist**: assesses the impact of ground conditions on development schemes such as tunnels, buildings, pipelines, docks, bridges and other structures.
» **Geoscientist**: locates and proves the existence of oil, gas, minerals and water reserves, estimating the extent and quality of the find.
» **Hydrogeologist**: identifies the type, distribution and structure of rock strata and their impact on the movement and accumulation of groundwater.
» **Minerals surveyor**: assists in planning mineral workings, ensuring the stability of mine sites and advising on the future restoration or redevelopment of exhausted sites.
» **Mudlogger**: based on an oil-drilling rig, collects and monitors information and samples from drilling operations to report back to drilling teams and oil companies.
» **Seismic interpreter**: interprets geophysical and geological data to produce maps of structures and to evaluate the prospect of recovering hydrocarbons.
» **Wellsite geologist**: supervises the logging of an oil or gas well, co-ordinates the collection and interpretation of well data and communicates the results to management and other colleagues.

Graduate jobs in which a degree in Geology could be useful
The following examples illustrate some areas of work that can give you
the opportunity to use the skills and knowledge gained from a Geology
degree.

» **Geographical information systems manager**: integrates a variety of
data into a relational database, which enables the user to integrate
spatial data into a topographical framework.
» **Hydrologist**: analyses water flow through pipes and channels for the
engineering and control of water. The focus of the work is on surface
water and it can include estimating yields of water and investigating its
quality.
» **Waste-disposal officer**: tasks could include managing a landfill site,
organising household-waste collection systems, including tendering for
contracts, and researching and implementing methods of toxic waste
disposal.

Further information
Careers advice for geologists – www.brookes.ac.uk/geology/geoljobs
Earthworks – www.earthworks-jobs.com
Geological Society – www.geolsoc.org.uk

Government and Politics

Students of this subject will learn about many different aspects of government and politics. Some of the questions that they may consider include:

» How have political systems changed over time?
» How do political structures and voting systems work?
» What is democracy and how does that concept differ according to different contexts and periods of history?
» What are the responsibilities of a Government and how do they exert their power?

Issues such as human rights, justice, war and peace may also be studied.

Main elements of the course
For an exact definition of the AS and A2 syllabus you will be studying, you should consult your school, college or the exam board itself. Some common elements of an A level course in Government and Politics include the following, although the titles of modules may vary according to the exam board:

» People and politics
» Governing in the UK
» The changing UK system
» UK political issues; introducing political ideologies; representation in the USA; introducing international politics
» The EU and European issues; other ideological traditions; governing the USA; issues in international politics

» Policy-making in the UK; ideological development in the UK; international politics in the UK.

AS candidates study and are assessed on 50% of the available modules; A2 candidates usually study all, or elements of all of them.

How is A level Government and Politics taught and assessed?

Teaching is mainly by classroom and textbook work but students may also look at news reports, political-party manifestos and many other politically related texts. Sometimes schools and colleges invite speakers to come and talk to students or visit political organisations. Assessment is mainly by written exams but there is an element of coursework.

Choosing other A level subjects to go with Government and Politics

This subject goes well with many others including English, History, Law, Business, Economics, Social Policy, Sociology and a few others.

Government and Politics at higher-education level

There isn't usually a requirement for Government and Politics A level for entry onto degree courses. Institutions usually ask for three good grades but some may prefer subjects in the arts and humanities.

A degree in Government and Politics?

Most university degrees are called BA Politics and, like many courses, usually have some core elements in the first year with some optional modules to make up the remainder of the second and third years. In many courses, optional courses may include:

» Comparative politics of Western Europe
» Politics of development
» History of political thought
» Advanced policy analysis
» Karl Marx
» Political leadership in the twentieth century
» Fascism
» Islam and the Middle East
» European Union
» Environmental policy.

Some courses may also involve some fieldwork, for which students spend some time at political organisations such as a political party or a pressure group, or go abroad to organisations such as the European Parliament, NATO or the European Commission.

Combining Government and Politics with other degree subjects

Politics goes well with subjects such as Law, Economics, History, Philosophy, Sociology, and modern manguages.

Foundation degrees and HNDs

There are some Politics-related Foundation degrees but none that focuses solely on the subject. There are some HNDs in Politics, but they mainly focus on law and administration and prepare people for careers in public administration or as a legal secretary.

Politics and your future career

Non-graduate jobs

There are a few jobs related to Government and Politics that students could go into straight after a Level 3 qualification. These include junior positions in the Civil Service or in local government. Additionally, the skills students gain from the course are transferable to many different areas of work.

Graduate jobs directly related to Politics and Government

There are very few careers in which a first degree in Politics is essential or directly relevant. There are some jobs closely related to a Politics degree, but they may also require relevant experience or further training. The following are most closely related to Politics:

» **Charity fund-raiser/charity officer**: entry for both types of work may initially have to be on a voluntary basis.
» **Political-party agent**: responsible for press coverage, publicity and liaison between the local party and the Member of Parliament.
» **Political-party research officer**: employed in a variety of settings, including higher education, political parties and independent agencies. Includes working for Members of Parliament and Members of the European Parliament.
» **Public-affairs consultant (lobbyist)**: represents the clients' case to those in Government who make decisions that affect them. The client may be a large company, a trade association, a pressure group or a local authority.

Graduate jobs in which a degree in Politics could be useful

» **Civil-Service fast streamer**: responds to the needs of individual departments, sometimes as a specialist in administration, finance or personnel. Assists in the formulation of policies and procedures, and co-ordinates their implementation.
» **Journalist**: responsible for gathering news and reporting work in both written and broadcast media. This involves developing contacts, interviewing people, attending press conferences and producing copy to a deadline.
» **Personnel officer**: responsible for advising on all policies relating to the use of human resources. Also responsible for the organisation and implementation of policies for workforce planning, recruitment, training, terms and conditions of employment and benefits.
» **Police officer**: first and foremost, graduates should be committed to the role of a police officer. Those with potential and continued high performance may be fast-tracked for promotion.
» **Public-relations account executive**: responsible for the transmission of positive information to particular audiences whose attitudes require influencing, using press and media liaison, company newspapers and journals.
» **Social researcher**: designs, formulates and carries out social research in a variety of settings including central and local government, independent research institutions and trades unions. This would only be appropriate if your degree scheme contains a component of research methodology.
» **Solicitor**: advises individuals and organisations on legal problems; prepares wills, contracts and other legal documents; researches and advises on points of law.

Further information
Civil Service Careers Page – www.civilservice.gov.uk/careers
Daily newspapers, especially the broadsheets
UK Parliament Homepage – www.parliament.uk

Health and Social Care (Applied A level)

This is one of the new Applied A levels recently introduced. The emphasis of this course is on the vocational contexts of health and social care. The course provides a pathway for candidates wishing to progress to higher-education courses in the area of health and social care as well as offering a useful introduction to employment in the sector. What are the most effective ways of caring for particular age groups? What is the role of exercise in the maintenance of good health? What are the career paths available in the health and social care field? These are just some of the questions that students of this course consider.

Main elements of the course

The outline below is based on what the main exam-board syllabuses include. For an exact definition of the GCE syllabus you will be studying, you should consult your school or college or even the exam board itself.

Courses generally include a mixture of compulsory units and some optional ones from a range of possible choices. The following units give an outline of the main areas covered:

» Caring for young people
» Caring for older people
» Caring for people with disabilities
» Complementary therapies
» Anatomy and physiology in practice
» Child and human development
» Nutrition
» Health and safety in care settings
» Promoting good health

» Health, illness and disease
» Diagnosis and treatment
» Working in health and social care
» Effective caring
» Effective communication.

How is A level Health and Social Care taught and assessed?

This subject is taught by a mixture of tutor-led activities, independent research and reading, and practical work. The context for this subject is very much work-related. Students may visit health and social care environments and schools or colleges may invite speakers in to talk about their work or current issues. Assessment is by a mixture of internal examination of prepared portfolios of work and by written exams marked by the exam board. Students don't need to have studied this subject previously but do need to demonstrate an interest in the area. At GCE AS level, single (three units) and double (six units) awards are available. At GCE A level, single (six units) and double (12 units) awards are available. Grades are awarded from A to E for both single awards and AA to EE for both double awards.

Choosing other A-level subjects to go with Health and Social Care

This subject could be combined with many subjects but ones that seem most compatible include Sociology and Social Policy, Government and Politics, Physical Education and Business Studies.

Health and Social Care at higher-education level

The A level course will give you a good understanding of the different career roles within the sector as well as further options at HE level. Students may opt for courses such as Sociology or Social Policy; others may be interested in courses such as Health Studies or Health Economics. Each course is different and you may need to have done specific subjects at GCE/Applied A level to gain a place. A course such as Health Economics would probably require an Economics background rather than one in Health and Social Care, for instance.

A degree in Health and Social Care?

There are many different options at university level and the whole area of Health and Social Care is usually broken down into specific areas, such as:

» Health studies
» Nursing studies

» Community health and nursing studies
» Community and youth studies
» Human services
» Primary care
» Social work.

Often these courses aim to give you a professional qualification in a particular area (eg social work) or are for currently experienced professionals who want to earn a degree. If you want a more academic course, you might want to consider degrees such as Social Policy, Health Care Policy, Sociology and others of a similar nature.

Combining a degree in Health and Social Care with other subjects
Combinations depend on the flexibility of where you're studying and your particular range of interests. But this degree subject may be combined well with other disciplines including Sociology, Social Policy, Politics, Public-Sector Administration, Biology and Management.

Foundation degrees and HNDs
There are many options for Foundation degrees in this area. In fact, there is much more choice at this level than in 'regular' degrees. Courses include Health and Social Care, Early Years, and Health and Social Care Management. Search for courses at www.ucas.com. In terms of HNDs, there are a number of options in specific aspects of Health and Social Care.

Health and Social Care and your future career

Non-graduate jobs
It is possible to get trainee posts in some areas of work in Health and Social Care without first getting a degree. These include jobs as care assistants, some areas of nursing and social care. It's also possible to find administrative positions in these environments (eg in the NHS or social services).

Graduate jobs related to Health and Social Care
If you want to be a doctor, then in most instances you would need three science subjects at A level or two sciences and A level Mathematics. Furthermore, for many professions allied to medicine, such as nurse, dietician, podiatrist or occupational therapist, it is necessary to complete a full vocational course from scratch. You would need to check entry requirements and funding. Other options closely related to Health and

Social Care also often require some further postgraduate training – see some of the examples below.

» **Health-promotion specialist**: promotes awareness of health issues to individuals and the community.
» **Health-Service manager**: responsible for the provision and commissioning of local healthcare, through the management of hospital, general-practitioner and community-health services. The National Health Service (NHS) offers graduate training schemes for these roles.
» **Lifestyle consultant**: provides physical fitness instruction and prescription of exercise/fitness programmes for individuals.
» **Nutritional therapist**: advises clients on how to improve overall health and wellbeing by assessing needs, problems, diet and lifestyle, and recommending changes.
» **Physiotherapist**: treats a range of health problems through massage, movement, exercise and technology. Although qualified status requires a further degree, posts as physiotherapy assistants are available, providing valuable experience.
» **Sports administrator**: the role varies depending on the organisation, but may include organising events, training sessions or conferences; marketing and public relations; producing literature; liaising with other agencies; financial and business administration.

Graduate jobs in which a degree in Health and Social Care could be useful

» **Charity officer**: the size of the organisation determines the responsibilities of this role. Besides administrative tasks, the position may include fund-raising, policy, public relations and education. Relevant experience, either voluntary or paid, may be necessary.
» **Civil-Service administrator, mainstream entry**: UK Home-Civil-Service departments employ administrators in a variety of roles, but tasks may include: organising services and resources, strategic planning, implementing policies, research and report writing.
» **Counsellor**: helps people cope with problems, decisions, transitions and crises. Usually needs voluntary and life experience. An accredited counselling qualification is often necessary.
» **Further-education lecturer**: delivering specific modules on, for example, relevant vocational training courses within post-compulsory education. Professional health qualifications could enhance your chances.

» **Local-government administrator**: responds to the administrative needs of individual departments. Assists in the formulation of policies and procedures.
» **Sales executive, medical**: represents pharmaceutical companies to general practitioners, retail pharmacists and hospital doctors.
» **Social worker**: aims to provide a service to individuals and families facing problems which they are unable to manage alone. Entry involves gaining work experience and a postgraduate course.

Further information
Jobs in community care – www.communitycare.co.uk
NHS Careers – www.nhscareers.nhs.uk
UK Civil Service Careers – www.civilservice.gov.uk/careers

History

History is seen as one of the more academic subjects. It develops lots of useful skills; the ability to critically evaluate written information, weighing up evidence and empathy are just some of the qualities History students learn to demonstrate. The study of History is not just learning about the past: it also involves thinking about how we view the past from today's perspective. The kinds of questions that students may consider include:

» What has been the global effect of the September 11 disaster?
» What are the ramifications of the reigns of prominent politicians and monarchs?
» What were the circumstances that led to the outbreak of World Wars I and II?
» How reliable are certain types of historical evidence?
» Why did Henry VIII split from the Catholic Church in Rome?

Main elements of the course

For an exact definition of the AS and A2 syllabus you will be studying, you should consult your school, college or the exam board itself. The main variations in History are in terms of the particular period that a school chooses for students to study as well as sometimes the type of history studied (ie social, political, or religious history). This course is also offered at AEA level by Edexcel exam board.

Most courses will cover the following:

» Significant historical events, issues or people
» A range of historical perspectives

» The diversity of society
» The history of more than one country or state
» A substantial element of English history
» Continuity and change over a particular period.

This is achieved in a variety of ways by different exam boards but a common pattern is as follows.

Document studies
As part of most A level courses, students are asked to examine documents from a particular period that they are studying. It could be a diary entry, a newspaper report, a poem, a prose extract or any other piece of text. Candidates are then asked questions on the document.

Periods of English history
Most A level syllabuses also include the study of a particular period of English history. This could be any period from 1000 to 1970. Particular courses tend to focus on up to 150 years at a time.

Periods of European and world history
Students may also have the opportunity to study a period of history other than British or English history. The same applies in terms of the length of period studied, but in general the periods offered for study for European or world history run from about 1000 to 1900 and nothing more recent than that.

Historically significant people
Some courses also offer the option of in-depth study of great historical figures. These could include any of the following:

» Charlemagne
» King John
» Philip II
» Elizabeth I
» Oliver Cromwell
» Peter the Great
» Napoleon I
» Lenin
» Stalin
» Chamberlain.

Historical themes
As well as studying individuals, some exam boards offer the opportunity to study certain historical themes. These could include any of the following:

» Rebellion and disorder in England 1485–1603
» The Catholic Reformation in the sixteenth century
» The decline of Spain 1598–1700
» War and society in Britain 1793–1918
» Civil rights in the USA 1865–1980.

Independent study
In some cases, students can do some independent study on a particular period, theme or historical figure as part of assessed coursework.

How is History taught and assessed?
Class lessons may also include practice in analysing historical documents, watching relevant historical programmes and group discussions. As with subjects such as English Literature, the volume of reading and writing is high in this subject and students should be prepared for that before they embark on the subject. Assessment varies with exam board: some may have final exams only; others have elements of assessed coursework, independent projects and open-book examinations.

Choosing other A level subjects to go with History
History is often combined with English Literature, Sociology, Geography, a modern language, Economics and Politics, but it can be taken with any subject.

History at higher-education level
Pure History remains a very popular choice at university level. Employers appreciate the skills that historians develop. You will often find that History forms a part of other degree subjects too. Related courses include Economic History, International History, Political History, Ancient History and many others. In general, you would probably need A level History to get onto these courses but this is not always the case.

A degree in History?
Like most degrees these days, History can be quite varied and flexible in its content. However, most degrees will have some core subjects (usually studied in the first year) and then have the option of allowing students to specialise in certain areas by choosing particular modules. The options usually include most areas of British, European and world history and

students will often consider issues such as theories of history as well as actual historical periods.

Combining History with other degree subjects

History is also combined with many other disciplines to form a joint degree. Such courses include: Geography and History, Politics and History, German and History and so on. The possibilities are endless because the vast majority of arts, humanities and social-science subjects at degree level always include a lot of emphasis on historical context, in this way, History is an ideal accompaniment for any of them.

Foundation degrees and HNDs

There is currently no separate History Foundation degree. Similarly, there is no HND in History, but there are some HNDs for which A level History would be good preparation. These include Heritage Conservation and Heritage Management.

History and your future career

Non-graduate jobs

Many employers requiring A levels do not really mind which subjects applicants have. In that sense, History A level is as good a choice as any. In fact, there may be some non-graduate areas of work where this A level is still more useful than some others because of the particular skills gained and knowledge acquired. These include:

» Administrative work (such as areas of the Civil Service)
» Management
» Sales
» Marketing
» Working as an assistant in a museum or gallery.

Graduate jobs directly related to History

History-related occupations include the following, but many require further education or training:

» **Academic librarian/information manager/records manager**: responsible for the acquisition, organisation and dissemination of information and materials within the library system or information unit.
» **Archaeologist**: studies human past through material remains.
» **Archivist**: acquires, selects, arranges, stores, preserves and retrieves records not in current use but deemed to be of historical value.
» **Genealogist**: traces and charts lines of descent or family trees. Possibility of freelance work.

» **Museum/art-gallery curator**: responsible for the care and improvement of a collection including exhibitions, catalogues and acquisitions.
» **Secondary-school teacher**: involved in teaching history to 11–18 year-olds in schools.

Graduate jobs in which History would be useful
The following represent some of the other potential areas of employment:

» **Arts administrator**: brings together artists and audiences to support and generate artistic activity.
» **Civil Service fast streamer**: through fast-stream entry graduates are involved in helping senior staff, and through them ministers, to formulate and implement policy. Graduates also enter as junior managers (formerly executive officers), with administrative and management responsibilities.
» **Journalist**: gathers and presents news and features to the public.
» **Primary-school teacher**: develops and fosters the appropriate skills and social abilities to enable the optimum development of children, within the framework of the National Curriculum.
» **Marketing executive**: manages the marketing of a product or service from research and development through to the launch. This can include promotion and advertising to the public or businesses.
» **Sales executive**: promotes and maximises sales of a company's products or services in designated markets. Also identifies new markets and new business and acts as liaison between producer and the retailer or wholesaler.
» **Solicitor**: advises individuals and organisations on legal aspects of personal and business problems.

Further information
Council for British Archaeology – www.britarch.ac.uk
Historical Association – www.history.org.uk
Museums Association – www.museumsassociation.org

History of Art

History of Art is a fairly specialised subject introducing students to a wealth of art, architecture and decorative arts from some of the world's most famous artists. In practice, most of these artists come from Western Europe and most are from the Italian Renaissance. As well as learning about some of the techniques used by artists, students learn about the historical, social, religious and political context in which the pieces of art were produced. What themes are repeated in art throughout the centuries? Which artists have been the most influential? How did the political hierarchy patronise artists to further their political ends?

Main elements of the course
The only exam board that currently offers this A level is AQA and the outline of the course is given below.

Module 1: ways of seeing
An introduction to the methodology and terminology of the history of art from c.1400 to the present day.

Module 2: birth and rebirth of Western art
Background knowledge of the Western tradition from Greek and Roman antiquity to the High Renaissance (c.1527)

Module 3: art of the modern world
Background knowledge of modern art, architecture and design from c.1850 until 1990.

Module 4: coursework project
Investigation of a topic of the candidate's choice.

Module 5: historical study 1
Candidates choose one topic from:

» Ancient Egyptian art and architecture
» Art and architecture in early-Renaissance Florence
» High-Renaissance Rome
» Baroque Rome
» English Baroque architecture
» The architecture, design and philosophy of galleries and museums
» The Gothic Revival.

Module 6: historical study 2
Candidates choose one topic from:

» Art and revolution (David, Gros, Ingres, Géricault, Goya, Delacroix)
» Eighteenth- and nineteenth-century Japanese prints
» Victorian narrative painting
» The Impressionist period
» Women in twentieth-century art
» Painting in Paris 1900–1914
» Figure, object, idea and installation – modern British art from c.1960 to the present day.

AS candidates study Modules 1–3, whereas A2 students study Modules 1–4, then choose one topic from Modules 5 and 6.

How is A-level History of Art taught and assessed?
This subject involves lots of looking at images in books, on slides, on stained-glass windows, in museums and in galleries. There may be visits to places of artistic/historical interest. There is also, of course, the usual classroom and textbook work, as with most other subjects. Students are also encouraged to do independent reading to support their learning in the classroom. Assessment is mainly by written exams, but Module 4 consists of a piece of coursework of approximately 3000 words.
There is no GCSE History of Art at present so you don't need that prior qualification, nor do you have to be good at art yourself. What's important is to have an interest in the subject and a willingness to learn.

Choosing other A-level subjects to go with History of Art
History of Art obviously goes well with History, Art and Design, English Literature and Classics. However, you can do this subject alongside

almost any other, as long as they satisfy the entry requirements for higher education, if that's what you decide to do.

History of Art at higher-education level

Most universities will not insist on A level History of Art, but they will prefer your subject choices to include English, History or a foreign language.

A degree in History of Art

A degree in this subject will really develop some of the themes explored at A level. Many courses include some fieldwork or visits to places relevant to the course. Examples of core and optional modules taken from a degree course are as follows:

Core modules

- Introduction to the history of art
- The classical tradition
- Theory and historiography.

Optional modules

- Impacts of the late antique c.350–850
- The art of Anglo-Saxon England, c.600–1066
- The age of the cathedrals: architecture in England c.1050–1250
- East and West: art of the crusading era
- European art of the High Middle Ages (art and patronage in fifteenth-century Florence; art in Venice – from Bellini to Tintoretto; the art of Holy Russia – painting, piety and power in the principality of Moscow c.1500–1680).

Combining History of Art with other degree subjects

History of Art is most commonly combined with English and History, and sometimes these are the only combinations that institutions offer. Sometimes, though, the subject can be combined with Classics, Archaeology or a foreign language.

Foundation degrees and HNDs

There are no Foundation degrees in this subject but there are some in the humanities-related field as well as in languages, literature and culture, which may include some references to the History of Art. There are currently no HNDs in this subject.

History of Art and your future career

Non-graduate jobs

It may be possible to get a starter position in an auction house, gallery, museum, design company or the antiques business straight after A levels, but increasingly some of these professions are being seen as graduate entry. But other areas are open to you too, and you don't have to think of history of art-related jobs only.

Graduate jobs related to History of Art

Most jobs directly related to the history of art require some form of further study, training or experience. Some of the jobs you could consider are listed below.

▣ **Auctioneer/valuer, fine arts**: identifies and values pieces of art, secures them for auctions and compiles catalogues. Also organises, attends and supervises auctions.
▣ **Historic buildings inspector/conservation officer**: inspects and reports on buildings of special architectural or historic interest to ensure their preservation and conservation.
▣ **Museum/art-gallery conservator/restorer**: assesses and analyses the condition of a particular type of object or art. Carries out treatments to arrest decay while maintaining the object's integrity.
▣ **Museum/art-gallery curator**: responsible for the development and management of a collection, including acquisitions, cataloguing and storage, as well as marketing and presentation to the public through exhibitions, documentation and talks.
▣ **Museum/art-gallery exhibitions officer**: researches, organises, selects objects for and mounts exhibitions in museums or art galleries.
▣ **Museum education officer**: creates a link between a museum and audiences and develops learning opportunities and materials for children or adults in or outside formal education.

Graduate jobs in which History of Art could be useful

▣ **Archivist**: manages a public or private collection of records (or images) of historical value by selecting, acquiring, cataloguing and preserving them.
▣ **Arts administrator**: supports, generates and is responsible for the organisation of artistic activities and organisations. Duties include budgeting and marketing.
▣ **Events organiser**: researches, organises and publicises events that allow businesses and customers to meet. Responsible for choosing venues and liaising with exhibitors, contractors, caterers and the press.

» **Heritage manager**: responsible for the conservation of and all aspects of public access to heritage sites. Develops and markets a site to visitors, while preserving its character.
» **Heritage officer/interpreter**: communicates the significance of a place or object to visitors through exhibitions, displays, re-enactments and publications.
» **Tourism officer**: develops and promotes tourist attractions to visitors and the tourism industry through events, marketing campaigns and information.

Further information

Association of Art Historians – www.aah.org.uk
Honour, Hugh and Fleming, John, *A World History of Art*, Laurence King Publishing, 2002
Institute of Conservation – www.icon.org.uk

Information and Communication Technology (ICT) (A level and Applied A level)

A level

The overall aim of this course is to encourage students to develop an understanding of the fundamentals of ICT and to provide the knowledge and skills suitable for participation in an evolving information-based society. The course provides a focus for developing these skills while ensuring that students acquire a sound knowledge of ICT. As a student of A level ICT, you are given the opportunity to develop interpersonal, academic and technical skills which will help you to meet career challenges in the future. What is an information system? How are ICT projects managed effectively? What is the most appropriate use of software for different purposes? These are just some of the questions that students of this subject are asked to consider.

Main elements of the course

For an exact definition of the AS and A2 syllabus you will be studying, you should consult your school, college or the exam board itself. All the exam boards cover the same topics but some of them are grouped together slightly differently. OCR is only offering ICT as an Applied A level from 2007. However, along with the other main exam boards, it does still offer A level Computing as a subject. This subject is much more technical than ICT. The main elements of most courses are:

Information, systems and communications
The building blocks of information systems.

Structured practical ICT tasks
Students learn practical skills in design, software development, testing and implementation.

Practical applications of ICT using standard/generic applications software

Students learn about standard applications software as well as online relational and non-relational databases.

Communications technology and its application

This aspect focuses on how ICT technology is used as a communication tool between individuals and businesses. Issues such as networking and further uses of ICT are explored.

ICT project

Students work on their own project throughout the course. This is usually an ICT solution to a problem encountered by a user.

ICT systems and systems management

This element of the course focuses in more detail on ICT and Communication systems for business as well as ICT solutions to many business problems.

AS students study two core modules and carry out a project. A2 students complete five modules and a project.

Applied A level

Applied A level ICT has many of the same elements as the traditional GCE course with a few differences. First, the applied course goes into more detail about some of the ICT functions/areas studied and how they can be applied in real life; second, students can take options with a more specialised vocational focus and a larger choice of options to choose from; and third, the assessment for the applied subject is based more on producing portfolios of evidence than written exams. The applied course is about how to do things rather than theoretical or historical considerations, as can be seen from the selection of modules below:

» Data handling
» Creating a website
» Publishing
» Advanced spreadsheet design
» ICT solutions
» Web management
» Programming.

How is ICT taught and assessed?

A level
You don't need to have any prior knowledge of ICT to study this subject at A level but a practical mind, an interest in the subject and good spatial awareness will help you. Teaching is via a mixture of classroom input and practical work in the ICT lab. Assessment is through written exams and a practical coursework project.

Applied A level
Teaching is similar to the traditional A level but there is a much more practice-based emphasis. Real-life case studies, visits to organisations using ICT in interesting ways and talks from ICT professionals are often part of the teaching methods used. Assessment is mainly by internally assessed portfolios of evidence with the occasional written exam. There are four possible routes for gaining an award in this subject: AS single award (three units); AS double award (six units); A level single award (six units); A level double award (12 units).

Choosing other subjects to go with A level ICT
Good supporting A levels for this one would include Business, Mathematics, Geography, Accounting, Computing and ICT and Design and Technology. However, you should make sure your focus isn't too narrow as this could affect your ability to get a place on an HE course.

ICT at higher-education level
Students don't necessarily need an A level in ICT to study it at a higher level but some universities may specify at least one scientific or technical A level. There are some courses based solely on information systems but they tend to be at postgraduate level. Some courses are very theoretical; others are very practical or applied in their emphasis. You should always check the specific nature of a course before applying.

A degree in ICT?
Most degree courses aren't called ICT but Computer Science or a variation thereof. Computing courses, even if they are theoretical, will consider how ICT is applied to business, industry and research. There are usually core components in the first year with some flexibility in the final two years depending on your interests. The kinds of issues considered include:

» Managing information systems
» Web and internet technologies
» Object-orientated software engineering

» Object-orientated modelling
» Communications and networks
» Logic programming
» Bioinformatics
» Information security
» Computational finance.

Assessment is via a combination of final exams, coursework and project work.

Combining ICT with other degree subjects
The different combinations possible with the subject are numerous, but some joint programmes offered by some ICT/Computer Science departments at university include:

» Computer Science with Management
» Computer Science with French
» Computer Science with Artificial Intelligence
» Computer Science and Physics
» Computer Science and Mathematics.

Foundation degrees and HNDs
There are many Foundation degrees in ICT-related subjects, examples being Business Information Technology, Web Development, Design for Digital Technologies and many more. Find a course at www.ucas.com. There are also a number of options at HND level that could be worth exploring.

ICT and your future career

Non-graduate jobs
Given that nearly every organisation needs computers now, you will be an asset if you have an advanced understanding of them. So in that sense, there are quite a few junior positions that you could apply for. You may even be able to get work in ICT support in some organisations without any further qualifications.

Graduate jobs directly related to Computing and ICT
Some of the more common job titles used include the following.

» **Applications developer**: writes and modifies programs to enable a computer to carry out specific tasks, such as stock control or payroll, typically for technical, commercial and business users.

» **Database administrator**: responsible for the usage, accuracy, efficiency, security, maintenance and development of an organisation's computerised databases.
» **Information-technology consultant**: gives independent and objective advice on how best to use information technology to solve business problems.
» **Software engineer**: specifies, develops, documents and maintains computer software programs in order to meet a client's or employer's needs. Usually works as part of a team.
» **Systems designer**: takes the specification for the requirements of a computer system and designs the system, including hardware, software, communications, installation, testing and maintenance.
» **Systems developer**: sets up the computer operating systems and standard software services essential to the operation of any computer.
» **Web designer**: responsible for the design, layout and coding of web pages. This is known as the 'front-end' of websites, as it is what the user sees. The work may also involve multimedia activities such as using video clips, music and other media. Web designers are also known as web producers, internet engineers and multimedia architects.

Graduate jobs in which Computing and ICT would be useful
Information technology is used in every single sector of the economy. The following jobs will make some use of your ICT background.

» **ICT-sales professional**: gives technical advice and guidance to customers pre- or post-installation of their computer systems; normally works in conjunction with sales representatives for a computer manufacturer.
» **Magazine journalist**: researches and writes news and feature articles suited to the magazine's reader profile.
» **Recruitment consultant**: particularly for the ICT sector. Obtains the brief for job vacancies from clients, then matches candidates with the relevant qualities to these vacancies and arranges interviews with the clients.
» **Secondary-school teacher**: teaches one, or more, specialist subject/s to classes of secondary pupils aged 11–18. ICT is currently a shortage subject.

Further information
British Computer Society – www.bcs.org
Computer Information Center – www.compinfo-center.com
Game On, advice on working in the computer games industry – ww.blitzgames.com/gameon

Latin/(Classical) Greek

Latin and Classical Greek are clearly not modern foreign languages like French or German in that they are not spoken any more. They are taught as separate subjects, even though they have much in common. The aim of studying these languages is to gain an insight into the culture of the classical world and all that it reveals about literature, language, philosophy, politics, religion and science. It is a fascinating subject to study. The study of Latin and Greek also gives students an excellent understanding of the English language and the origin of many of its words and phrases. There is usually an element of translation involved, so students need to gain a good understanding of the original languages.

Main elements of the course
OCR is the only board offering Greek and Latin A levels. The following outline is based on its syllabuses.

Both the Latin and Greek courses have the following features:

» A study of the language, including grammar, syntax, declensions and other aspects
» A study of set texts from classical literature including the epics, tragedy, comedy and historical texts
» Translation work.

Students studying for AS Latin or Greek must take two core modules and one optional unit. A2 students take four core modules and two optional units. Latin is also offered at AEA level by OCR exam board.

How are A level Latin and Classical Greek taught and assessed?

Given that these languages are not spoken any more, there is much emphasis on understanding the language in its written form, so students do a lot of reading and writing. Occasionally, there may be visits to places of classical interest to support the knowledge gained in the classroom. Students need not have studied these subjects at GCSE level, but it certainly helps! Assessment is by various types of written exam including translation and comprehension papers.

Choosing other A level subjects to go with Latin and Classical Greek

Other subjects that complement these subjects include Ancient History, Classical Civilisation, History, Literature, modern foreign languages and English Language. If you want to study at a higher level, always check universities' admission criteria before choosing your subjects.

Latin and Greek at higher-education level

Some universities offer single Honours Latin or a combined course in Latin/Greek at degree level. To study these subjects at HE level, you must have studied them at A level. Many others, however, offer Classics, which is an in-depth study of the languages and literatures of ancient Greece and Rome.

A degree in Latin/Classical Greek?

At this level, students extend their knowledge of the language learned at A level and study more of the literature of Rome and Greece. Some students prefer to study Classics, which has a little more emphasis on the context of the time and a little less on the language, although the ability to understand the language is still very important. Most universities have core modules in the first year with some options later on in the course.

Combining Latin/Greek with other subjects

These subjects go very well with subjects that also investigate the classical world, such as Classics, Ancient History, English Literature, Philosophy, Politics and even Law. In practice, however, possible permutations of combinations depend on the attitude of the academic departments.

Foundation degrees and HNDs

There are currently no Foundation degrees or Diplomas in this subject. You may be interested in related subjects in the humanities, however.

Latin/Classical Greek and your future career

Non-graduate jobs
This A level will give you lots of marketable skills for a variety of jobs, even though you probably won't be able to use the knowledge you've learned. Skills you can gain from this course include the ability to research, think logically and analyse information, and empathy.

Graduate jobs related to Latin/Greek
There are only a few jobs directly related to a Latin/Greek degree. For the following occupation a degree in a classical subject is essential.

» **Secondary-school teacher**: there are a few Postgraduate Certificate in Education (PGCE) courses for graduates wanting to teach Classics in state secondary schools. Opportunities also exist in primary schools, independent schools, sixth-form colleges and further or higher education.

Graduate jobs in which Classics would be useful
Jobs in which the transferable skills learned from a Classics background are particularly useful include the following.

» **Administration**: planning and organising services, providing information and collecting data to form the basis for future actions within the organisation, and informing the world outside the organisation. You could work in public service, industry (company secretary), education, health service, charities, voluntary or international organisations.
» **Archivist**: preserves, stores and safeguards records for permanent retention. Makes records accessible for administrative or historical research purposes. Latin is necessary for work with older archives.
» **Civil Service fast streamer**: involves policy making (administrative trainee) or general management (staffing, finance, immigration, consular work) roles in embassies or high commissions abroad, and in the Foreign and Commonwealth Office in London.
» **Museum/art-gallery curator**: the collection, documentation, preservation, display and interpretation of materials for public benefit.
» **Solicitor**: prepares deeds and contracts of all types, manages legal cases, instructs counsel (ie barristers) in the higher courts and acts as an advocate for others in the lower courts. You could work in private practice as a generalist or specialist, in industry, public service, law centres, magistrates' courts or the armed services.

» **Technical author**: preparing technical information for publication in a way that is intelligible to a wide range of users. You need to produce clear, logical, unambiguous and accurate text.

Further information
Barrow, R H, *The Romans*, Penguin
Joint Association for Classical Teachers – www.jact.org
Sowerby, R, *The Greeks*, Routledge

Law

A level Law gives you a good insight into how the English legal system operates. It examines how laws come into being and how they are upheld. As well as the systems of law and justice, students are introduced to the many different types of law that are practised in the UK as well as their implications for everyday life. Students may also engage with some important and interesting issues such as human rights, euthanasia, the impact of EU legislation on our lives and much more.

Main elements of the course
For an exact definition of the AS and A2 syllabus you will be studying, you should consult your school, college or the exam board itself. Four out of the five exam boards offer this subject and cover more or less the same ground – differences are mainly in how the material is organised and what the modules are called. The following outline is based on the AQA syllabus.

Law making
This module introduces students to the different legislative processes and bodies, including parliaments and assemblies in the UK as well as European legislative bodies.

Dispute solving
How legal disputes are resolved, including an introduction to the work of the courts, judges, magistrates, solicitors and barristers, and how legal advice is financed.

Concept of liability
The basics of criminal liability, issues surrounding property, sanctions and punishments.

Concepts of law
Issues explored here include: law and morals; law and justice; balancing conflicting interests; fault; judicial creativity.

Criminal law (offences against a person) and contract law
A2 students choose one module from either criminal law (offences against a person) or contract law.

Criminal law (offences against property)/tort/human rights/ consumer protection law
A2 students choose one module from one of the four areas above.

As usual the AS course is 50% of the A2 course, with AS students studying the first three options and A2 students studying the first four modules and choosing one option from the remaining two units.

How is A level law taught and assessed?
Students don't have to have studied GCSE Law to do well at this subject because A level Law is essentially learning a lot of facts about the legal system and then analysing what is learned. There is a lot of reading and writing for this subject – as there is when working as a lawyer! – but don't let that put you off because it is a fascinating subject. All the work is assessed by exams at various points in the course and there is no coursework assessment for this subject.

Choosing other subjects to go with A level Law
Law goes well with many other subjects, including arts and humanities subjects such as English and History. It also goes well with other finance-related subjects such as Accounting, Business and Economics. Many students also study Law alongside a modern foreign language.

Law at higher-education level
Most universities do not require you to have studied A level Law to study it at higher-education level, but they will look for sound traditional subjects. In some respects, if you want to study Law at university, you may be safer choosing traditional academic subjects rather than more business-focused ones, even though the practice of law is largely a commercial affair.

A degree in Law
A Law degree is usually called LLB Laws (Bachelor of Laws) and it will cover the basics in the first year, expanding what is taught at A level. In

the second and third years, students have the chance to take some more specialised units aligned to their personal or career interests. Core courses at university level usually include:

» Elements of contract law
» Criminal law
» Public law
» European law.

Special options could cover a whole range of law-related topics, but the following is a small sample:

» Banking law
» Medical law
» Russian legal institutions
» International trade law
» Human rights law
» Copyright and designs.

Combining Law with other degree subjects
This really varies from university to university, but some common combinations include:

» Law and Accounting
» Law and Philosophy
» Law and a Modern Foreign Language
» Law and Sociology
» Law and Business.

Foundation degrees and HNDs
There are some Law and law-related Foundation courses available, which you can find at www.ucas.com. Edexcel currently offers an HND in Business Law.

Law and your future career

Non-graduate jobs
Law is seen by employers as an academically sound and rigorous subject and therefore students with this subject under their belt will be in demand. However, it's also important to emphasise other transferable skills such as problem-solving, analytical skills and writing skills. Jobs working in law are mainly reserved for graduates but you may be able to work in junior positions in legal contexts such as administration in a law firm.

Graduate jobs related to Law

» **Solicitor/Barrister**: requires postgraduate qualifications and training.

Jobs in which a degree in Law would be useful
There are a number of careers in which legal knowledge and skills can be put to use.

» **Advice worker**: employed by local and central government and the voluntary sector. Advice and information is provided to the public or to special client groups, in person, in writing and over the telephone.
» **Ancillary legal professions**: if you are attracted to work in the legal field you could consider an ancillary role. A law degree is not required and postgraduate qualifications are not necessary for all of them. Occupations include barrister's clerk, legal executive (England and Wales), licensed conveyancer and legal secretary.
» **Chartered accountant**: works to ensure effective use of financial resources of individuals or organisations. Can include auditing, financial management and planning, and giving financial advice.
» **Civil Service fast streamer**: employed in all government departments. Some have legal responsibilities, eg Lord Chancellor's Office, CPS.
» **Excise and inland customs officer**: involves regulating the entry of certain goods through ports and airports; controlling the movement of dutiable materials within the UK and the assessment and collection of VAT.
» **Immigration officer, passport control**: meets passengers and assesses their eligibility for admission.
» **Inspector of health and safety**: inspects factories, quarries, offices, farms and other places of work. Ensures working conditions and machinery are safe and comply with regulations.
» **Local-government administrator**: employed in all departments in local authorities.
» **Police officer**: maintains law and order; protects persons and property; prevents crime; deals with emergencies.
» **Prison officer**: keeps people committed by the courts in custody; looks after them with humanity, and helps them lead law-abiding and useful lives in custody and after release.
» **Probation officer**: supervises people placed under probation orders and other forms of supervision, and those released from custody.
» **Tax inspector**: determines the tax liabilities of individuals and businesses on behalf of the Inland Revenue, including assessment and examination of accounts.

» **Trading-standards officer**: promotes, maintains and develops fair trading through inspecting premises, advising traders and consumers, and investigating complaints.

Further information

Bar Council – www.barcouncil.org.uk
Law Careers Advice Network – www.lcan.org.uk
Law Society – www.lawsociety.org.uk

Leisure Studies (Applied A level)

This is one of the new Applied A levels and has a number of aims: to give students an insight into the leisure industry within the UK and EU; to equip students with some of the skills and techniques to enable them to develop a career in the leisure industry; and to encourage an understanding of the benefits of a healthy and active lifestyle. It is ideal for those students who want a broad background on the leisure and recreation industry, and the course will allow them to progress to further and higher education or employment. This sector is a fast-growing one. People have more disposable income to spend on leisure and recreation than ever before (the number of health clubs is at a record high) and the industry needs well-qualified people.

Main elements of the course
The exam boards that offer this subject cover very similar ground. The main differences are the title of modules and the way the material is organised and structured. The following outline is based on the AQA specification.

- Unit 1: the leisure industry today
- Unit 2: a people business
- Unit 3: getting it right in the leisure industry
- Unit 4: leisure facilities
- Unit 5: lifestyles and life stages
- Unit 6: leisure organisations
- Unit 7: fitness training for sport
- Unit 8: leisure in action
- Unit 9: working in the people business
- Unit 10: current issues

» Unit 11: leisure and the media
» Unit 12: lifestyle management
» Unit 13: leisure in the community
» Unit 14: outdoor leisure.

How is A level Leisure Studies taught and assessed?

You need no prior knowledge of this subject to take this course; however, having studied GCSE Leisure and Tourism may be an advantage. As well as classroom work, students may visit different types of leisure and recreation organisations and do lots of independent research about the sector. Assessment is by a combination of externally set and marked written exams and internally assessed portfolios of evidence. For instance, your assessment task for a unit may be to write a report, carry out an investigation or sit a written exam. There are four possible routes for gaining an award in this subject: AS single award (three units); AS double award (six units); A level single award (six units); A level double award (12 units).

Choosing other A level subjects to go with A level Leisure Studies

This subject goes well with other applied subjects such as Business Studies, ICT and Travel and Tourism. If you would like to study Leisure Studies *and* Travel and Tourism, be aware that there may be too much overlap between the subjects and exam boards may therefore not permit this combination – you need to check with the exam board first before choosing both subjects.

Leisure Studies at higher-education Level

There are different types of leisure- and recreation-related degrees such as Leisure and Recreation Management, Sports Science, and Recreation and Leisure Studies. Check the entry requirements for each course as there may be quite a bit of variation between them. Many courses are sandwich courses, meaning that students work for a year in the leisure and recreation industry at some point during their course. Some courses offer a year-abroad option.

A degree in Leisure Studies?

The most common type of degree in this area is Leisure (and Recreation) Management. Sometimes it is taught by the Business School of a university and sometimes not. Such a course would usually include:

» Leisure analysis and information technology
» Foundations of leisure
» Leisure business

» Leisure policy
» Leisure facility management
» Sport industry
» Sport tourism.

Combining Leisure Studies with other degree subjects

This depends on individual departments, but possible joint subjects include: Business/Management, Accounting, Nutrition, Sports Science, Computing and possibly a few others.

Foundation degrees and HNDs

There are many Foundation degree courses and HNDs available in this area and students often choose this route rather than going for traditional 'academic' degrees.

Leisure Studies and your future career

Non-graduate jobs

There is a great demand for staff in this ever-changing sector and therefore it's possible for students with an A level in the subject to start working at junior supervisory levels in a variety of settings. As well as knowledge gained from the course, students need to emphasise their skills in teamwork, problem solving and using initiative. As their careers develop, students may want to consider vertical progression through a relevant HND course or something at an equivalent or higher level.

Graduate jobs related to a degree in Leisure and Recreation

» **Betting-shop manager**: responsible for running a betting shop profitably, organising, recruiting and training staff, security and for ensuring fast and accurate payment of winnings.
» **Fitness-centre manager**: responsible for day-to-day running of the business, design of activity programme, budgeting, customer care, market research and marketing, membership sales, and staff supervision, development and training.
» **Leisure-centre manager**: promotes, organises and runs a leisure centre in either the public or private sector. Effectively in charge of several small business operations: catering, personnel, customer relations, bars, promotions and financial planning.
» **Lifestyle consultant**: carries out fitness assessments, provides physical fitness and lifestyle-health programmes in mainly private-sector

health clubs or hotels, but sometimes in organisations wishing to provide facilities for their employees.

- **Outdoor-pursuits manager**: responsible for provision of facilities and instruction in a range of outdoor activities. Duties include: staff management; health and safety of clients; planning day and evening activities; handling customer complaints.
- **Sports administrator**: works within a sport's governing body or the Sports Council, dealing with financial, organisational and administrative aspects of their sport. May involve national travel to support events.
- **Sports-development officer**: encourages people to take part in sport by promoting their sport to target groups. Usually works for a governing body or professional association.
- **Theme-park manager**: involves recruiting staff, dealing with finances, ensuring high standards of presentation and service, marketing the park and liaising with other management staff.
- **Tourism officer**: plans and co-ordinates leisure activities, usually on a geographic basis for a local authority.

Graduate jobs in which a degree in Leisure and Recreation could be useful

- **Events organiser**: organises conferences/events/exhibitions, liaises with clients, is responsible for administration, and manages staff and contractors.
- **Further-education or higher-education lecturer**: teaching through lectures, tutorials and practical-skills classes on (aspects of) leisure and recreation.
- **Newspaper journalist**: responsible for news or information gathering and reporting. Involves developing contacts, interviewing personalities, attending press conferences and producing copy to a deadline.
- **Public-relations officer**: promotes events, sponsorship deals and presents sport-and-leisure topics to the media.
- **Retail manager**: specialist sports-retail companies could offer management posts in buying, merchandising or store management.

Further information
Fitness Industry Association (FIA) – www.fia.org.uk
Institute of Leisure and Amenities Management (ILAM) – www.ilam.co.uk
Institute of Sport and Recreation Management (ISRM) – www.isrm.co.uk

Mathematics

Mathematics is at the core of many of the things we know about life, about the world around us, even the movements of substances inside our bodies. What's the best way of predicting the likelihood of something happening? How fast is a particular planet spinning? How does the economy work in detail? How much profit will a company make? Trying to answer any of these questions will to a certain extent involve the use of numbers and mathematics. This subject builds on the basics learned at GCSE as well as introducing new concepts and new ways of solving particular problems. Students should be aware that GCE A/AS level Statistics is also available for study.

Main elements of the course

For an exact definition of the AS and A2 syllabus you will be studying, you should consult your school, college or the exam board itself. This course is also offered at AEA level by Edexcel exam board.

Mathematics is really divided between 'pure mathematics' and 'applied mathematics' (applying the subject to different contexts and uses). The exam boards tend to give schools and colleges some choice about the options students choose in the different mathematical areas. The main areas of the syllabuses are as follows:

Pure mathematics
This is the foundation for what you do in other areas and includes topics such as trigonometry, quadratic equations, vectors, differential equations, complex numbers and matrices.

Mechanics
This focuses on the way objects move and looks at physical forces. Topics studied include Newton's law of motion, linear momentum,

centre of mass, equilibrium, energy, work and power, elasticity, and inertia.

Statistics and probability

Collecting and presenting data, working out valid sample sizes from a group of data, probability, variables, mean value and spread, and hypothesis testing.

Discrete mathematics

Discrete mathematics is used in computer science, management, and economics and includes things such as algorithms, networks, linear programming, game theory and dynamic programming.

Those studying for the AS award generally take three units and those going for the Advanced award take six units.

How is A level Mathematics taught and assessed?

To do well in this subject, students realistically need to have achieved a grade A or B at GCSE level. This is partly because a sound grasp of previously learned concepts is needed in order to make real progress at A level. There is a lot of class work, with students learning new theories and then doing practice examples. There is also lots of using graphs and charts, equations and calculator work. Coursework is an option for this course, otherwise it is all assessed through written examinations.

Choosing other A level subjects to go with A level Mathematics

Mathematics goes well with subjects such as Physics, Chemistry, Business, ICT/Computing and Biology. However, it is often combined with other subjects such as a modern foreign language or Music.

Mathematics at higher-education level

To study Mathematics at a higher level, you will need to have achieved a good grade at A level in the subject. Degree courses may focus on different areas of mathematics such as pure mathematics or applied mathematics.

A degree in Mathematics?

Most degree courses have core modules and optional elements. A sample is given below.

» **Sample core courses:** Calculus, Geometry, Introduction to Dynamical Systems, Linear Methods
» **Sample optional courses:** Financial Mathematics; Quantum Mechanics; Space-Time Physics; Thermodynamics and Information Theory

Combining Mathematics with other degree subjects
Common joint degrees offered by universities include: French and
Mathematics, Mathematics and Philosophy, Mathematics and Physics,
Mathematics and Management, and Mathematics with Computer Science.

Foundation degrees and HNDs
There are no Foundation degrees or HNDs in Mathematics, but there are
some in related areas such as Engineering and ICT.

Mathematics and your future career

Non-graduate jobs
Mathematics is a very attractive subject to employers as there aren't
many organisations that don't have to do some kind of mathematical
work. It could be possible to get junior positions in retail, banking,
insurance and many other areas straight after A levels.

Graduate jobs related to Mathematics

- **Actuarial work**: an actuary studies past events to predict future
  outcomes. This often involves the application of probability and
  statistics to financial affairs, especially life assurance, pensions and
  social security.
- **Economic and statistical work**: a statistician collects, analyses and
  interprets quantitative information. This work is carried out in many
  organisations and research establishments, notably the Civil Service,
  the Health Service and large industrial and commercial organisations.
- **Scientific research and development**: most openings are for applied
  mathematicians with relevant higher degrees, including Information
  Technology. Much of the work is carried out in multidisciplinary teams
  with other scientists.
- **Secondary-school teacher**: you will normally have to undertake a
  Postgraduate Certificate in Education (PGCE) before entering this field.

Jobs in which a degree in Mathematics could be useful

- **Accountancy**: employers of trainee accountants rarely specify degree
  disciplines, but all look for numeracy and literacy skills and the capacity
  to establish interpersonal relationships rapidly.
- **Insurance and pensions**: insurance companies offer many openings in
  addition to actuarial work, including investment analysis, systems
  technology and underwriting.
- **ICT, economics, statistics and management services**: the
  employers of computer personnel are numerous, with the three main

openings being found with users of the equipment, eg banks, oil companies and retail chains.

» **Management consultancy**: covers a wide range of applications and the type of work depends on the sector. Competition for posts is fierce.

» **Retail banking and personal financial services**: The growth in applications of information technology has led to an increase in careers for graduates in areas covering communications, data processing and funds transfer.

Further information

Institute of Mathematics and its Applications – www.ima.org.uk
Mathematics Careers – www.mathscareers.co.uk
Royal Statistical Society (RSS) – www.rss.org.uk

Media: Communication and Production (Applied A level)

This course aims to provide candidates with knowledge, understanding and experience of the media and the practical skills to work in the sector. Students will study the working methods of current practitioners in the media and gain an understanding of the range of roles within the different areas of the media.

Students will learn about what the mass media is and how it works in all its forms, focusing on audio-visual material. This knowledge is used to research and create students' own media products, mainly working in the audio-visual area by making and editing their own videos.

Main features of the course
The exam boards cover the same ground in this subject; the differences lie in the presentation of the modules and how they are grouped together. For an exact definition of the AS and A2 syllabus you will be studying, you should consult your school, college or the exam board itself. The outline below is based on the Edexcel course.

Unit 1: industries, texts and audience
In this module students learn different ways of looking at and analysing the media, using ideas like narrative, representation and ideology.

Unit 2: skills development in media
This unit develops the practical skills needed to create a video and printed publicity material for a video.

Unit 3: media production brief
This module uses the skills and knowledge learned in Units 1 and 2 to prepare and create a moving-image product.

Unit 4: researching for media production
In this module students develop an idea for a video product, and do some research into how viable the idea is from a professional and commercial point of view.

Unit 5: media production project
Students make a film or video, and are expected to show very detailed evidence of how the production process was planned, using industry-standard documentation techniques.

Unit 6: professional practice in the media industries
This module develops students' knowledge of how media production works in different media industries as well as the moral, legal and ethical context of the industry.

How is A level Media taught and assessed?
No prior knowledge is needed for this course but candidates must have a good standard of literacy, some creative flair and an interest in the sector of work. Teaching is by a combination of classroom work, talks by people in the media field, possible work experience opportunities and practical work. Students may also spend a lot of time working with different media (eg print, TV, film, photography and so on). Assessment is via a combination of external examination and portfolios of evidence.

Choosing other subjects to go with A level Media
This subject could go with almost any other subject but if you want to study this subject at a higher level, then remember to check institutions' entry criteria so you know which subjects to choose.

Media at higher-education level
It's possible to study Media at a higher level in a variety of contexts including HNDs, Foundation degrees and Bachelor's degrees at universities. The important thing to remember is that some courses are very academic or theoretical, whereas others are more vocationally specific.

A degree in Media?
At university level, degrees in Media can come in many different forms. On the one hand, they can focus on a very specific area of media (eg digital media, media production, print media, television media, interactive media and so on); on the other hand they can be general media-related degrees such as Media Studies or Media Arts. An example of some options in a university Media Arts degree is given below:

» Women's cinema
» Postmodern film and television
» Modernism
» Media and history: the Holocaust
» French cinema
» Hollywood star performances
» Television genre.

Combining Media with other degree subjects

Media is often combined with subjects such as English, a modern foreign language, ICT and many others.

Foundation degrees and HNDs

There are many different Foundation degrees available in specific areas of media. You can search for them at www.ucas.com. There are also a number of HNDs in media-related subjects including Media (audio) and Media (journalism).

Media and your future career

Non-graduate jobs

A level in Media will give you good skills and an insight into the profession. The media profession is notoriously difficult to get into though, and you have to be prepared to make contacts and often work on an unpaid basis to build experience until you get your first break. Non-media careers are still open to you, of course.

Graduate jobs related to Media

Many students on these courses are interested in gaining employment in all aspects of the media industry. Careers in the media, however, are highly sought after and competition is likely to be fierce.

» **Broadcast assistant, radio**: assists with production and presentation of programmes for local and national radio stations.
» **Broadcasting presenter**: fronts the programme; specific responsibilities vary depending on the programme.
» **Journalism**: reports on news and other areas of interests for newspapers, periodicals, radio and TV.
» **Multimedia programmer**: researches, develops and produces materials for new-media-based company activities.
» **Programme researcher, broadcasting/film/video**: acts as an assistant producer with responsibility for conception and implementation of a programme.

- **Radio producer**: responsible for initiating ideas, selling these to commissioning editors and managing the technical and creative teams to produce the final programme.
- **Television/film/video producer**: undertakes the artistic interpretation of materials and directs the production of shows/films.
- **Television production assistant**: provides organisational and secretarial services for programme director.

Graduate jobs in which a degree in Media could be useful

- **Advertising account executive**: takes overall responsibility for co-ordination, planning and organisation of advertising campaigns.
- **Arts administrator**: acts as facilitator for the exhibition and preservation of cultural forms including performing, visual and heritage arts.
- **Events organiser**: identifies potential business, researches, writes, plans and runs all types of conference on behalf of a client or his/her own organisation.
- **Information officer/manager**: ensures effective communication of information relating to a particular field of interest.
- **Market-research executive**: undertakes systematic research to determine the potential market for a product or service.
- **Public-relations account executive**: PR agencies work for their clients in presenting their image to the public. They decide on strategies to be used and which media would be the most effective.

Further information

British Film Institute – www.bfi.org.uk/education
Media studies website – www.englishandmedia.com
O'Sullivan, Tim *et al, Studying the Media*, Hodder Arnold, 1998
Skillset – www.skillset.org; www.skillsformedia.com

Media Studies

This course enables candidates to develop a critical awareness and understanding of the media and its role in influencing society. It also examines the institutions which produce media products and the audiences which respond to them. A distinctive feature of the A level Media Studies courses is the practical production element at both AS and Advanced GCE stages. This enables candidates to put theory into practice by creating their own media products, giving them opportunities to engage in creative and imaginative activities. There is also an emphasis on textual analysis in this course, more so than in the Applied A level in Media.

Main elements of the course

AQA, WJEC and OCR offer a Media Studies GCE A level. Edexcel offers a GCE A level course in Media: Communication and Production. The courses cover very similar ground, but vary in the titles of the modules and how they are organised. The following outline is based on the AQA specification.

Module 1: reading the media

This course introduces students to key concepts to be applied when analysing the media. Concepts include: media representations; media institutions; media language; media values and ideology; and media audiences.

Module 2: textual topics in contemporary media

Using the concepts learned in Module 1, students study two media texts by close analysis. Candidates choose two texts from four areas: broadcast film and fiction; documentary; advertising and marketing; British newspapers.

Module 3: practical production

Students apply what they've learned so far and produce a media production, using at least two different media.

Module 4: texts and contexts in the media

Students choose a further two media texts to study from the areas of: the production and manufacture of news; representations; genre; media audiences.

Module 5: independent study

Students research an independent area of study that will deal with a contemporary text, topic or issue.

Module 6: comparative critical analysis

Students have to explore the similarities, differences and themes across different media genres.

Students for AS Media Studies take modules one to three, whereas students going for the full A level study all six units.

How is A level Media Studies taught and assessed?

Students of this course do a lot of close textual analysis so a GCSE in English Literature, Language or Media Studies is very helpful, and some schools and colleges may insist that you have it. As well as classroom reading and writing, teaching will also be carried out by asking students to analyse different media such as video, film, TV and newspapers. Assessment is by a combination of written exams and coursework.

Choosing other A level/Applied A level subjects to go with A level Media Studies

A level English Literature and/or English Language would go well with this subject, as would Communication Studies, Film Studies and perhaps a modern foreign language. If you want to study this subject at a higher level, always check with universities and colleges which subjects they prefer you to have under your belt. Also check with your school or college about overlap between subjects that have a lot in common, eg Film Studies and Media Studies – sometimes exam boards don't allow too much overlap.

Media at higher-education level

It's possible to study Media at a higher level in a variety of contexts including HNDs, Foundation degrees and university Bachelor's degrees.

The important thing to remember is that some courses are very academic or theoretical, while others are more vocationally specific and aim to improve your chances of getting a job in the field.

A degree in Media?

At university level, degrees in Media can come in many different forms. On the one hand, they can focus on a very specific area of media (eg digital media, media production, print media, television media, interactive media and so on); on the other hand they can be general media-related degrees such as Media Studies or Media Arts. Some are vocational, some are academic, some are a mixture of the two. An example of some options in a university Media Arts degree is given below:

» Media practice
» Women's cinema
» Postmodern film and television
» Modernism
» Media and history: the Holocaust
» French cinema
» Hollywood star performances.

Combining Media with other degree subjects

Media is often combined with subjects such as English, a modern foreign language, ICT and many others.

Foundation degrees and HNDs

There are many different Foundation degrees available in specific areas of media. You can search for them at www.ucas.com. There are also a number of HNDs in media-related subjects including Media (Audio) and Media (Journalism).

Media and your future career

Non-graduate jobs

An A level in Media Studies will give you good skills and an insight into the profession. The media profession is notoriously difficult to get into, though, and you have to be prepared to make contacts and often work on an unpaid basis to build experience until you get your first break. Non-media careers are still open to you, of course.

Graduate jobs related to Media

Careers in the media are highly sought after and competition is likely to be fierce.

- » **Broadcast assistant, radio**: assists with production and presentation of programmes for local and national radio stations.
- » **Broadcasting presenter**: fronts the programme; specific responsibilities vary depending on the programme.
- » **Journalism**: reports on news and other areas of interests for newspapers, periodicals, radio and TV.
- » **Multimedia programmer**: researches, develops and produces materials for new-media-based company activities.
- » **Programme researcher, broadcasting/film/video**: acts as an assistant producer with responsibility for conception and implementation of a programme.
- » **Radio producer**: responsible for initiating ideas, selling these to commissioning editors and managing the technical and creative teams to produce the final programme.
- » **Television/film/video producer**: undertakes the artistic interpretation of materials and directs the production of shows/films.
- » **Television production assistant**: provides organisational and secretarial services for programme director.

Graduate jobs in which a degree in Media could be useful

- » **Advertising account executive**: takes overall responsibility for co-ordination, planning and organisation of advertising campaigns.
- » **Arts administrator**: acts as facilitator for the exhibition and preservation of cultural forms including performing, visual and heritage arts.
- » **Events organiser**: identifies potential business, researches, writes, plans and runs all types of conference on behalf of a client or his/her own organisation.
- » **Information officer/manager**: ensures effective communication of information relating to a particular field of interest.
- » **Market-research executive**: undertakes systematic research to determine the potential market for a product or service.
- » **Public-relations account executive**: PR agencies work for their clients in presenting their image to the public. They decide on strategies to be used and which media would be the most effective.

Further information

British Film Institute – www.bfi.org.uk/education
O'Sullivan, Tim *et al*, *Studying the Media*, Hodder Arnold, 1998
Skillset – www.skillset.org; www.skillsformedia.com

Modern Languages

There are many modern languages that can be studied at A level including French, German, Spanish, Italian, Portuguese, Urdu, Chinese, Dutch, Gujarati, Persian and quite a few more. The study of a foreign language at A level not only allows you to communicate with people from other countries, it also gives you an insight into the cultures and histories of the countries where the language is spoken. If you study French, for instance, you could also end up studying Impressionist painting or other aspects of France's history or culture. If you enjoy communicating, learning new words and have a talent for remembering things, then an A level in a modern language could be for you.

Main elements of the course
Some foreign languages are offered at AEA level by different exam boards: French (OCR); Spanish (Edexcel); German (CCEA).

Irrespective of the language you choose or the exam board your school or college uses, your syllabus will include the following elements.

Speaking
You will be expected to converse in the language and learn new vocabulary including verbs. You may also have to take part in role plays. In the oral exams, you may have to make a presentation.

Listening
Students often find the listening part of learning a new language difficult. Throughout the course, you will listen to the language in different contexts such as news reports, song lyrics and conversations.

Reading
You will also have to do a lot of reading of different types of materials: this could be newspapers, literary texts, business letters, emails and so on.

Writing
The kind of writing skills you may need to develop as part of this A level include judging the right form and tone for a particular piece of written communication, as well as ensuring it is grammatically and linguistically sound. Tasks such as writing a reply to a letter, making a job application or writing a promotional leaflet may all be included.

Aspects of culture and society
Some foreign-language courses also include a separate element on learning about the culture and society of the country where the language is predominantly spoken. This could be related to literature, the environment, the media, healthcare issues and many other topics.

How is an A level in a modern language taught and assessed?
To do well at A level languages you will probably need a good grade (A or B) in the language at GCSE because students need to build on what they've learned previously (although it's not impossible to start some courses from scratch as long as you have some previous knowledge of the language). Teaching is via a combination of conversations in the language, written exercises, listening to the language and reading practice. Assessment is by a combination of written exams, oral exams, listening exams, reading comprehension and a small element of coursework.

Choosing subjects to go with an A level in a modern language
You may choose to study more than one language at A level or you may wish to combine your one language with a different kind of subject. Languages go well with almost anything, but popular combining subjects include English Literature, History, Music, Business, Law and Mathematics.

Modern languages at higher-education level
You may wish to study the language on its own, in combination with literature, or the literature alone. Unless you are a native speaker, in the vast majority of cases you will need a good A level grade in the subject you wish to pursue at university.

A degree in a modern language?

As well as degrees in specific languages (and literatures), many institutions offer a degree in combined modern languages. To get onto one of these courses, you often have to have studied two languages at A level. On the whole a degree in a modern language will require a very high degree of competence in the language and will be much broader in its scope than the subject at A level. Sample modules from a French degree course could include:

» Language, communication and society
» Landmarks: reading the classics of French literature
» French: the linguist's view
» Cinema in France
» Advanced French linguistics
» Textual revolutions: writing in nineteenth-century France.

Combining modern languages with other degree subjects

Studying a modern language jointly with another degree subject is a very popular option. It's quite common to see combinations with English, Politics, Mathematics, History, Classics, Music, Anthropology, Travel and Tourism, Management, Law and many others.

Foundation degrees and HNDs

There are a few Foundation degrees related to modern languages. They are often combined with specific vocational areas such as tourism. There are no HNDs in modern languages.

Modern languages and your future career

Non-graduate jobs

Languages are a desirable asset at any level of employment. If you want to go into work straight after A levels, you could try approaching companies who do business with foreign countries or target tourism industries such as airlines, travel agencies and tour operators. You may start at only a junior level but there isn't so much of a graduate culture in these sectors so you should be able to progress quickly if you are good at your job.

Graduate jobs related to modern languages

There are a few jobs in which modern languages are central to the work. These include translation and interpreting, teaching modern languages, some areas of journalism and some areas of work in the Diplomatic Service. In many cases, however, the languages you have learned are secondary to the main skills and knowledge needed for the job. Having said that, they can often come in handy later on in your career, so it's important not to let your skills get too rusty.

Graduate jobs in which a degree in a modern language could be useful

- **Buying/purchasing**: promotes and negotiates sales of products or services to customers worldwide.
- **Diplomatic Service**: most posts abroad involve dealing with representatives of overseas governments, explaining British foreign policy and negotiating over different issues or, in some cases, promoting exports and assisting trade.
- **Distribution/logistics manager**: co-ordinates the supply, movement and storage of goods and raw materials, including operational management.
- **Marketing**: analysing market information and promoting products worldwide with a view to achieving optimum market share and profitability.
- **Publishing and printing**: initially you are likely to be recruited into sales, marketing, production, finance, editorial or administration. Over a third of the books published in the UK are sold overseas.
- **Solicitor**: even in the UK, solicitors' services are offered in 22 languages and many big commercial firms have offices in trading nations worldwide.
- **Teacher of English as a foreign language**: teaching English to foreign students either in the UK or overseas.

Further information
Centre for Information on Language Teaching and Research (CILT) – www.cilt.org.uk
Institute of Linguists – www.iol.org.uk
Institute of Translation and Interpreting – www.iti.org.uk

Music

A level Music offers you the opportunity to develop the performing, composing and listening skills you gained at GCSE level. The course will also introduce students to a wide variety of music, particularly from the western classical tradition and jazz, but students are also expected to do their own performing and composing and there is a considerable amount of freedom in choosing the style, genre or repertoire. In essence, this course is for those who want to develop a career in music or simply for those who want to deepen their appreciation of music.

Main elements of the course

For an exact definition of the AS and A2 syllabus you will be studying, you should consult your school, college or the exam board itself. Whichever exam board your school uses, the course will include the following elements: performance; history of music; listening comprehension; composing; and understanding the mechanics of music. The following outline is based on the AQA specification.

Module 1: understanding music

Students learn about musical language and context by studying set works in certain historical periods (eg 1700–1850) and different genres of music (eg musicals, church music, reggae and so on).

Module 2: composing

Students compose two pieces of music, one of which has to be performed as part of the next module.

Module 3: performing
Students prepare and perform a programme of ensemble music, lasting between five and ten minutes using the voice or a musical instrument. They also perform the piece that they composed for module two.

Module 4: understanding music
Students learn more about musical language and context by choosing to study a set work from the twentieth- and twenty-first-century options.

Module 5: investigation, report and composition
This module allows candidates to do independent research on two works connected by genre, place or occasion but separated in time by at least 100 years. Students then produce a report on their findings and produce a composition in the style of one of the pieces.

Module 6: performing
Solo performance on one instrument/voice of the candidate's choosing lasting between seven and ten minutes.

Candidates for the AS award study modules one to three and A2 students complete all six modules.

How is A level Music taught and assessed?
A good grade at GCSE music is usually required in order to study this subject at A level. Teaching is by listening to musical works, reading about the history of music, and the practical work of composing and performing. Students can usually play an instrument, which they will probably need to practise in their own time. Assessment is by examination, performance and coursework.

Choosing other A level subjects to go with Music
Music goes well with a whole range of subjects including the humanities, Literature, ICT/Computing and even Mathematics. Other subjects, such as Practical Music and Music Technology, complement Music well, but they will not be accepted if you want to study single Honours Music at higher-education level.

Music at higher-education level
You will need A level Music to study it at a higher level. Music is usually offered as a single subject or jointly with another subject. It's not offered by every institution, but many universities are increasingly trying to position themselves as centres of excellence or specialist centres for Music.

A degree in Music?

Like most degrees, Music usually includes both compulsory modules and some specialist modules that you can choose later on in the course. A degree in this subject will allow you to go into much greater depth than you did at A level and of course you will be able to develop even further your skills in listening, composition and performance. A typical Music degree could include the following modules:

» Historical topics
» Principles of tonal music
» Studies in contemporary music
» Techniques of composition
» Practice and theory of performance
» Introduction to world musics
» Musical techniques
» Issues in theory and analysis
» Notations of western music
» Special study
» Composition
» Musicology
» Performance
» Options from a whole range of subjects such as film music, Mozart's piano concertos, music, politics, ideology, Viennese modernism, etc.

Combining Music with other degree subjects

Universities offer combinations depending on the structure of their own academic departments, but typical combinations include: Music with a modern foreign language, Music with Management, Drama and Music, History and Music, Mathematics and Music.

Foundation degrees and HNDs

There are some Foundation degrees in Music and music-related areas. There are some HNDs available in Music Performance and Production.

Music and your future career

Non-graduate jobs

It's hard to go into a musical career with A level Music alone, but it could give you a head start in terms of showing your interest in and knowledge of music. As long as you are prepared to work your way up from the bottom, it's quite possible to find junior roles within radio, a music magazine or a record company.

Graduate jobs related to Music

Even graduate jobs can be difficult to obtain because of the competitive nature of the industry and the relatively small number of openings. Jobs most closely related, either directly after graduating or after further training and work experience, include the following:

» **Composer**: writes original music, often commissioned by a third party. Very few musicians derive all their income from composition: an average proportion of income from composing would be 20%, with the other 80% usually made up from teaching or performing.
» **Editorial assistant**: assisting in the production of manuscripts and textbooks for music teaching. All the music publishers in the UK are small employers who recruit music graduates only occasionally and expect them to start at the very bottom.
» **Magazine journalist**: there are many specialist publications covering all aspects of music. However, the field is extremely competitive and it may be necessary to work freelance, and undertake training in journalism.
» **Music librarian**: responsible for the acquisition and promotion of library music resources within the community, in education or within a private company. Graduates need to qualify as a professional librarian first before being able to specialise in a field such as music.
» **Music therapist**: using music to treat, educate or rehabilitate people with emotional, physical or mental problems; based in hospitals, schools, prisons, etc.
» **Musical performance/festival organiser**: employed on a small scale by orchestras, opera or ballet companies and concert halls. May also be employed by companies, conference centres and arenas to host and organise big music festivals such as Glastonbury, the Reading Music Festival and many others.
» **Musician**: most musicians are self employed and accept a wide range of engagements. These can include orchestral, ensemble or solo work in the classical field and also in clubs, cruise liners and cabaret in the popular music area.
» **Private music teacher**: involved in teaching music in schools for all ages, both in the state and independent sectors. Some are employed as peripatetic teachers working in a number of schools in an area and are employed by the LA's music service.

Graduate jobs in which a degree in Music could be useful

» **Arts administrator**: acts as facilitator for the presentation, exhibition or preservation of cultural forms, including the performing arts. Administrators are employed on a small scale by orchestras, opera or ballet companies and concert halls.

- **Community-arts worker**: concerned with the promotion of the arts in the community, often through working with young people out of school hours.
- **Film/video production manager**: working on programmes in radio, television or for video production and post-production. This is a very popular area but difficult to break into, even if you are prepared to start at the bottom.
- **Museum/art-gallery curator**: there are occasional openings for curators and assistants of musical collections in the major museums following the appropriate postgraduate training.

Further information

British Society for Music Therapy – www.bsmt.org
Head, L, *The British and International Music Yearbook*, Rhinegold Publishing
Royal Academy of Music – www.ram.ac.uk

Music Technology

This course allows students to study music through technology and equips them with the skills needed to use technology to make music effectively. It also shows students what an incredible impact technology has had on music, in particular the components of digital technology. While there is some overlap with A level Music, in that students learn about musical traditions (eg Western classical music and jazz), the emphasis is always on how technology is used in relation to those traditions or styles. There is also a greater emphasis on analysing modern popular music.

Main elements of the course
Edexcel is the only exam board currently offering this course. A brief outline of the syllabus is given below:

Unit 1: the development of technology in music
This module focuses on how technology has affected music and how technology can be used to compose and perform music. Students become familiar with the language and terms of music technology and learn about specific technologies such as MIDI sequencing.

Unit 2: music from the Western classical tradition
Students learn about the historical context of this musical tradition and how it has influenced contemporary performers and composers. This unit also explores how technology has been used to interpret music from this tradition.

Unit 3: popular music and jazz

This module introduces students to pop and rock music as well as jazz written from the beginning of the twentieth century to the present day. Students learn about the structures of the music and the musical methods used, with particular reference to technology.

Unit 4a: music for the moving image

This unit is about how music has been written for TV and film as well as the musical methods and structures involved. This is done in relation to core 'texts' such as *Pyscho*, *Titanic*, *Robin Hood Prince of Thieves*, and *Planet of the Apes*.

Unit 4b: words and music

This module examines the relationships between words and music and the historical influence on them. This is done in relation to 'core albums' such as Elton John's *Captain Fantastic and the Brown Dirt Cowboy*, Queen's *A Night at the Opera*, Peter Gabriel's *Us* and Pink Floyd's *Dark Side of the Moon*.

The course also includes practical work in listening, composition and performance. As usual, A2 candidates do the full syllabus and AS candidates do half of it.

How is A level Music Technology taught and assessed?

A good grade in GCSE Music is usually required in order to study this subject at A level. Teaching is by listening to musical works, reading about the history of music, and the practical work of composing and performing. Students on this course will be using technology a lot so they should be comfortable with that. Assessment is by written examination, performance and coursework.

Choosing other A level subjects to go with Music Technology

Music Technology goes well with a whole range of subjects including the humanities, Literature, ICT/Computing and even Mathematics. Other subjects such as Music and Practical Music are also good complements. Music Technology (without regular Music A level) will often not be accepted as a way of getting onto a degree course in Music.

Music Technology at higher-education level

There are a few options for you to pursue Music Technology at a higher level. As well as HNDs and Foundation degrees, there are a few universities that offer Music Technology as a degree course. For these courses you will probably need A level Music or Music Technology.

A degree in Music Technology?

There are not a huge number of Music Technology degrees available, but this is changing and over the next few years there will be more courses of this nature. The kinds of things you could study at degree level include:

» Techniques of digital audio
» Creating and performing
» Digital cultures
» Making musical forms and structures
» Creative sound recording and production
» Contemporary composition and aesthetics
» Programming for creative music technology.

Combining Music Technology with other degree subjects

Universities offer combinations depending on the structure of their own academic departments, but typical subject partners include:
ICT/Computing, modern foreign languages, Management, Drama, History, Mathematics.

Foundation degrees and HNDs

Music Technology is available both as a Foundation degree and as an HND. There are also some HNDs available in Music Performance and Production.

Music Technology and your future career

Non-graduate jobs

It's hard to get into a musical career with A level Music Technology alone but it could give you a head start in terms of showing your interest and knowledge of music. As long as you are prepared to work your way up from the bottom, it's quite possible to find junior roles in radio, with a music magazine or a record company.

Graduate jobs related to Music Technology

The explosion in modern communications technologies makes digital music central to contemporary media – from music and sound design for film and video to live performance, interactive games, multimedia, music and audio tools for the internet, and from broadcasting work in television and radio production and advertising, location and studio sound engineering, to original composition in popular and classical music genres. So as well as traditional music jobs (see the entry under A level

Music), these kinds of jobs are also open to graduates of Music Technology.

Further information

British Society for Music Therapy – www.bsmt.org
Head, L, *The British and International Music Yearbook*, Rhinegold Publishing
Royal Academy of Music – www.ram.ac.uk

Performing Arts (Applied A level)

This course, one of the new Applied A levels, is about giving students a thorough insight into the performing-arts sector and equipping them with the skills and knowledge needed to enter into the many different employment areas in the field and/or to apply for courses in higher education. The aspects of the performing-arts industry that students can learn about include: dance; drama; music; music technology; arts administration and marketing; technical and production aspects of performance. Students interested in dance should be aware there is an AS/A level offered solely in this subject.

Main elements of the course
The outline below relates to the syllabus set out in the OCR guidelines. There will be some variation in relation to different exam boards but the same content is more or less covered.

Unit 1: investigating performing-arts organisations
This module involves looking at, for example, cinemas, theatres, dance halls and stage schools and learning about the different job functions that exist within them.

Unit 2: professional practice: skills development
In this module students produce a skills development plan either for performance (eg dance, acting, music, etc) or for production (eg lighting, make-up, arts administration, etc).

Unit 3: professional practice: performance
Here students put into practice the skills that they have learned by conducting a performance for a group.

Unit 4: professional practice: production
In this module students put their skills into practice by putting on a production.

Unit 5: getting work
This provides an introduction to the different careers and further study options within the sector and the main skills needed to succeed in the field.

Unit 6: exploring repertoire
This module allows students from both the production and performance pathways to get together in order to produce a piece of drama.

Unit 7: producing your showcase
A synoptic module in which students can show all the skills they've developed over the course.

Unit 8: production demonstration
Here students produce a piece of work in response to a brief set by the teacher.

How is A level Performing Arts taught and assessed?
You need no prior knowledge of this subject to take the course, but an interest in the topic as well as career motivation in the area are advantages. As well as classroom work, students may visit different types of arts-related organisations, and do lots of independent research about the sector. Assessment is by a combination of externally set and marked written exams and internally assessed portfolios of evidence.

Choosing other A level subjects to go with Performing Arts
Subjects that go well with Performing Arts include English, Media, Music Technology and many others.

Performing Arts at higher-education level
There are a few courses available at degree level that cover many aspects of performing arts, but the majority tend to specialise in one or two areas. Decide which part of performing arts you excel in and go for that. This is also a popular subject at Foundation degree level.

A degree in Performing Arts?
There are a few degrees that cover the broad subject of performing arts as a single degree without specialising in one particular area. Some of the areas a degree might cover include:

» Performing arts: contemporary practice
» Dance in education
» Film, text performance
» International theatre since 1945
» Music in education
» Storytelling and poetry in performance
» Performance in virtual worlds
» Arts in the community
» The film industry.

Combining Performing Arts with other degree subjects

This subject goes well with Music, a modern language, English, ICT/Computing, Media and countless others.

Foundation degrees and HNDs

There are HNDs in areas such as Dance Production, Music Production and Performing Arts. There are also a number of Foundation degree courses in many different aspects of performing arts. You can search for them at www.ucas.com.

Performing Arts and your future career

Non-graduate jobs

If you want a career in performance or in the technical side of performing arts, you will probably have to do further study. It's possible to get your foot in the door straight after your A levels, though, by working in an administrative role in a theatre or opera house, for example in the box office.

Graduate jobs related to Performing Arts

Some related jobs will require relevant postgraduate study and if you want to become a performer you may need further professional training.

» **Actor**: using speech, body language and movement, an actor communicates a character and situations to an audience.
» **Dancer**: working in a variety of genres, from classical ballet and West-End musicals to contemporary dance and freestyle (disco), a dancer's role may also involve education or therapy, as well as entertainment.

» **Primary-school teacher**: teaching younger children the full range of curriculum subjects.

» **Secondary-school teacher**: teaching drama, music or other curriculum subjects in schools and colleges.

Jobs in which a degree in Performing Arts could be useful

» **Arts administrator**: facilitates the planning and promotion of visual and performing-arts activities, sometimes specialising in areas such as finance and marketing.

» **Community-arts worker**: concerned with the promotion of the arts in the community often through working with young people in schools and youth centres.

» **Dramatherapist**: using drama to treat or educate people with health or emotional difficulties through therapeutic techniques.

» **Editorial assistant**: music degrees may enable entry to specialist fields concerning manuscripts or new music.

» **Journalist**: there are many specialist publications covering the arts but entry is very competitive. Graduates could start in mainstream broadcast or print journalism and specialise or become freelance later.

» **Programme researcher**: supports the producer by helping to organise and plan the programme.

» **Television production assistant**: organises and co-ordinates programme activities, booking performers and facilities and providing administrative support.

Further information

Council for Dance Education and Training – www.cdet.org.uk
Incorporated Society of Musicians – www.ism.org
National Council for Drama Training – www.ncdt.co.uk

Philosophy

Philosophy literally means 'the love of wisdom'. The discipline of philosophy has been around for a very long time, as far back as the ancient Greeks, and remains popular today. The kind of wisdom that is studied varies enormously but in general includes questions about the meaning of life, the nature of reality, consciousness, how to live a good life, questions of ethics and much more.

Questions that philosophers could ask include:

- Do we really exist?
- Why are there wars?
- If we are controlled by genes and DNA, are we responsible for our choices?
- Can discrimination ever be justified?

The successful study of philosophy requires an analytical, logical mind, a curiosity about the world, and the ability to look at things from different points of view.

Main elements of the course

For an exact definition of the AS and A2 syllabus you will be studying, you should consult your school, college or the exam board itself. The main variations in Philosophy are in terms of the particular philosophers and 'strands' of philosophy that a school chooses for students to study. However, most exam boards stipulate that students should gain an appreciation of the major elements of philosophical thought.

A broad outline of a Philosophy A level syllabus could look like the following:

Theory of knowledge

This focuses on questions such as 'What do we know?' and 'How do we know it?' The nature and extent of knowledge are fundamental issues in this subject: it raises questions regarding the beliefs we have, how we acquire them and whether we can take them to be knowledge.

Moral philosophy

This aspect of philosophy covers ethical questions such as 'What makes our actions right or wrong?', 'What is best for society?' and 'Are there any fundamental moral truths or are there simply different opinions and values?' Different types of ethics are studied as part of moral philosophy.

Philosophy of religion

This aspect of the subject asks one of the biggest questions of all: 'Is there a God?' and goes on to discuss religious concepts and claims, including the rationality of the belief in God, whether it can be proved that God exists, and if he does, what does that mean for us?

Philosophical set texts

Most courses also include the study of certain core or key philosophical set texts. Typically, these would include some of the following:

» Plato: *Republic*
» Descartes: *Meditations*
» Marx and Engels: *The German Ideology*
» Sartre: *Existentialism and Humanism*
» Mill: *On Liberty*
» Aristotle: *Nicomachean Ethics*
» Hume: *An Enquiry Concerning Human Understanding*
» Nietzsche: *Beyond Good and Evil*
» Russell: *The Problems of Philosophy*
» Ayer: *Language, Truth and Logic.*

Philosophical themes

As well as core texts, this subject is also studied along the lines of themes. The following themes are the most common:

» Philosophy of mind
» Political philosophy
» Philosophy of science.

Independent study

In many cases, students are required to carry out an extended essay on a particular philosopher or philosophical theme.

How is Philosophy taught and assessed?

Philosophy is taught by a mixture of students' independent learning and classroom work. To get the very top grades, students are encouraged to read around the subject to support the knowledge they gain in class. Class lessons may also include the discussion of philosophical concepts. As with some other subjects, the volume of reading and writing is high in this subject, and students should be prepared for that. Furthermore, becoming familiar with philosophical concepts and terms can be difficult at first.

The method of assessment varies according to the exam board: some may have final exams only; others have elements of assessed coursework, independent projects and open-book examinations. Think about how you perform best before you choose your particular course.

Choosing other A level subjects to go with Philosophy

Philosophy is an interesting subject because it touches on science, law, religion, history, literature and mathematics as well as politics. In this sense, any A levels could be good to have as a combination. This subject would be widely accepted as one of the supporting A levels for entry to most degree courses, unless a particular course requires all science or mathematics-related subjects.

Philosophy at higher-education level

It's not necessary to have an A level in Philosophy to study it at a higher level. This is partly because the subject is not widely available as an A level choice at schools and colleges.

A degree in Philosophy?

Although most university Philosophy courses include (usually in the first year) an introduction to the main strands of the discipline, the content can vary widely. Some focus on more traditional forms of philosophy such as Plato and Aristotle; others place their emphasis on applying philosophy to contemporary issues in politics, law, religion and society in general.

Possible options outside core modules could include the study of particular philosophers such as Wittgenstein or Hegel; the study of philosophy by country of origin such as Indian Philosophy and Greek Philosophy; or the study of certain 'schools' of philosophy such Marxism (named after Karl Marx) and aesthetics (the study and appreciation of beauty and art).

Combining Philosophy with other subjects

Because the study of Philosophy cuts across so many other disciplines, it is quite common to see this subject being combined with both arts and sciences. A very well-known combination or joint degree is Politics, Philosophy and Economics (PPE) offered by some universities. However, combinations with History, modern languages, Theology, Mathematics, Physics, Literature and Classics are pretty common too.

Foundation degrees and HNDs

Given that Philosophy is not a vocational subject, there aren't any specific diplomas or Foundation degrees in it. There are, however, some related areas that students could be interested in considering if they have enjoyed A level Philosophy, such as an HND in Legal Studies.

Philosophy and your career

Non-graduate jobs

Philosophy is not a vocational subject, so it will not lead directly to a particular career. Undoubtedly, it does develop some very useful skills such as critical thinking, the ability to create a persuasive argument, independent thinking, good judgement and logic. These could be useful for a range of jobs such as administration, some government work and some junior aspects of managerial work.

Graduate jobs in which Philosophy would be useful

Careers include those which require strong analytical and communication skills:

- **Advertising account planner**: analyses consumer response to advertisements and helps to integrate this into advertising strategy; evaluates the effectiveness of advertising.
- **Civil Service/local-government administrator**: assists in the formulation of policies and procedures in a government department or local authority, and co-ordinates their implementation.
- **Information-technology consultant**: gives independent advice to clients on ICT solutions to business problems; analyses problems, makes recommendations and develops and implements new systems.
- **Marketing executive, consumer products**: assists in the development of brands and the promotion of fast-moving consumer goods (FMCG) and products to the public.
- **Newspaper journalist**: reports on news and other items of current interest for newspapers.

▣ **Personnel officer**: advises on all policies relating to human resources in an organisation, including employee planning, recruitment, pay and conditions of work, training and welfare.

▣ **Political-party research officer**: employed in a variety of settings, including higher education, political parties and independent agencies. Includes working for Members of Parliament and Members of European Parliament.

▣ **Public-affairs consultant (lobbyist)**: represents the clients' case to those in government who make decisions that affect them. The client may be a large company, a trade association, a pressure group or a local authority.

▣ **Publishing copy/sub-editor**: ensures that a manuscript is accurate, appropriate for intended readership, has a consistent style and a logical structure for the publisher before it goes to the production stage.

▣ **Solicitor**: advises individuals and organisations on legal problems; prepares wills, contracts and other legal documents; researches and advises on points of law.

▣ **TV programme researcher**: generates programme ideas, researches background material, and briefs production teams and presenters.

Further information

Nagel, Thomas, *What Does it all Mean?*, OUP
Royal Institute of Philosophy – www.royalinstitutephilosophy.org
Russell, Bertrand, *The Problems of Philosophy*, OUP

Photography

A level Photography combines the theoretical and practical aspects of the subject. You will gain an insight into both the history and development of photography and the different types of photography. You will also be introduced to the techniques of photography (both lens-based and digital) and how to take photographs effectively. Syllabuses may also include an exploration of how the way a photograph is taken influences the interpretation of the viewer.

Main elements of the course

The exam boards that offer this subject usually categorise it under 'Art'. The kind of topics that students would study include the following:

Lens-based photography

Printing and developing films; using lenses, equipment and formatting; working in the darkroom; lighting and exposure techniques.

Experimental photography

Students are encouraged to experiment with different darkroom techniques such as using: pinhole cameras; photograms; solarisation; multiple exposure; and reversal printing. You may also look at alternative processes such as liquid emulsions, toning and art papers.

Film and video

Scripting; editing; production; direction.

Multimedia

You will learn about computer-based and camera-based processes relating to video, audio, animation and digital imaging.

If you're studying for the A2 award you will take six units relating to these areas. If you're going for AS, then you will only have to do three. Check the exam-board syllabuses for an exact definition.

How is A level Photography taught and assessed?

Many students who choose this subject have studied Art at GCSE level. This is not necessarily a prerequisite, but you should at least have some basic knowledge and interest in the area. There is a lot of practical work, some of it independent, in this subject. Assessment is by a combination of assessed practical work and an assessed portfolio of evidence.

Choosing other A level subjects to go with Photography

To study art-related subjects at degree level you will need a good portfolio of work. Choosing art-related subjects to go with Photography may help you with this. Subjects such as Art and Design, Media, Media Studies and Communication Studies could help, but be careful there's not too much overlap between subjects – it may affect your chances of entry into higher education. If you want to be a freelance photographer, then maybe choosing Business Studies at A level could help your cause.

Photography at higher-education level

There are degree courses in Photography, but they are often run at specialist 'arts' colleges, sometimes combined with other related subjects or forming part of a larger subject. To get onto a course you will need a portfolio of work as well as relevant A levels or equivalent. Some students opt to take a Foundation degree first.

A degree in Photography?

The first year of a degree course is usually directed by staff, and during this time you'll establish a solid understanding of camera, darkroom and studio skills, including digital applications. Projects and seminars examine the ways in which the camera generates content and how meaning is constructed. The second year explores cultural meaning and context. Your studies are often supported by guest lectures from leading photographers, art directors and curators. By the third year, you'll be encouraged to follow your own interests, and you may have to exhibit your work at the end of the degree programme.

Combining Photography with other degree subjects

Combining Photography with subjects such as Video, Film, Communication Studies or Media Studies will broaden your portfolio. But to make a success of being a self-employed photographer, it could be a good idea to combine your degree with Business Studies if possible.

Foundation degrees and HNDs

There are a few Foundation degrees available in Photography and photography-related areas. You can search for these at www.ucas.com. Edexcel currently offers an HND in Photography.

Photography and your future career

Non-graduate jobs

To be a freelance photographer you don't necessarily need a degree as long as you have a portfolio and as long as you take photographs that are of interest to people. Many self-employed photographers make money from taking wedding photographs; others sell their pictures to newspapers and journals. Many do a combination of many things. You may be able to start off in the sector working in a photography shop or as an assistant to a professional photographer.

Graduate jobs in which a degree in Photography could be useful

As well as jobs related to photography and journalism, graduate jobs in which a degree in Photography could be useful include:

- » **Advertising art director**: creates visual ideas to be used within advertising. Works as part of a team alongside illustrators, photographers and those responsible for editorial. Can involve any media.
- » **Museum/art-gallery curator**: acquires, cares for, stores and presents a collection of artefacts or works of art in order to inform, educate and entertain the public. May include other elements such as public relations, fund-raising and customer care.
- » **Picture researcher/editor**: finds suitable images for print and electronic publications. Investigates copyright, negotiates fees, liaises with clients. Part-time and distance-learning courses are available.
- » **Visual merchandiser**: creates window and interior displays in shops and department stores with the aim of increasing sales.

Further information

Association of Photographers – www.the-aop.org
British Institute of Professional Photographers – www.bipp.com
British Journal of Photography online – www.bjphoto.co.uk

Physical Education (PE)

A level PE develops students' knowledge, understanding and skills in many areas. Firstly, as an A level PE student you would learn about specific physical activities and sports and develop the skills of planning, performing and evaluating these activities. But you would also get an insight into the historical and social context of sport as well as the relationship between psychology and physiology in sport. This is both an academic and a practical subject!

Main elements of the course

For an exact definition of the AS and A2 syllabus you will be studying, you should consult your school, college or the exam board itself. The following outline is roughly based on the Edexcel syllabus.

The social basis of sport and recreation

This unit seeks to investigate the historical and cultural basis of sport in order to develop an understanding of the current role and provision of sport in modern society. The unit also includes an investigation into the social factors that influence both performance and participation.

Enhancing performance

Students carry out a number of activities or sports and learn how to improve in these areas as well as how to measure the improvement.

Exercise and training

The unit will advance students' understanding of anatomy and physiology and build on this through the principles and methods of training.

Global trends in international sport
Students undertake a comparative investigation of sport and recreation in a number of differing regions. These have been grouped together in broad geographical groups. The requirement is to identify trends and systems in similar countries.

Refining performance
This builds on previous units of enhancing performance and exercise and training.

Scientific principles of exercise and performance
This unit advances students' knowledge of exercise and training, and provides an introduction to energy systems, sports psychology and mechanics.

AS level students complete three of these modules and A level students complete all six.

How is A level PE taught and assessed?
By its very nature, PE is not a classroom-bound subject. There will be the usual classroom note-taking but you will also spend a lot of time engaging in various types of physical activity, games and sports. Assessment is by a combination of written exams, coursework and assessed practical activities.

Choosing other A level subjects to go with PE
Subjects that may go well with PE include: Applied Leisure and Recreation, Computing/ICT, Biology and Psychology. If you want to study Sports Science at degree level, you may want to choose two sciences to go along with PE.

Physical Education at higher-education level
There are courses in PE at higher-education level but they are often linked with teacher-training courses because PE is still often seen as a school subject. Higher-education courses in Sports Science are more common. Institutions sometimes express a preference for sciences at A level rather than PE, so always check in advance!

A degree in PE/Sports Science?
A degree in this subject will explore the area in greater depth and breadth while offering you some options to specialise in. A sample of degree modules could look like the following:

» Fitness and training
» ICT for sport-and-exercise science
» Nutrition
» Structural kinesiology
» Sociology of sport
» Sport and exercise pedagogy
» Physiology of exercise and health.

Combining PE/Sports Science with other degree subjects

This can be combined with almost any other subject, depending on your preferences and the flexibility of academic departments. Common combinations include:

» Sports Science with Management
» Chemistry and Sports Science
» Mathematics and Sports Science
» Physics and Sports Science
» Geography and Sports Science
» English and Sports Science.

Foundation degrees and HNDs

Edexcel offers HNDs in Leisure as well as Sports and Exercise Sciences and there are many Foundation degrees available related to Sports Studies and Sports Science. Visit www.ucas.com to search for these.

PE/Sports Science and your future career

Non-graduate jobs

It's possible to get into a few sports-related areas without a degree. These include junior positions in sports clubs and gyms, as well as administrative roles within a hotel and leisure complex. With some further training, although not necessarily at degree level, it's even possible to become a personal trainer/coach. Of course, other non-sports jobs are open to you too.

Graduate jobs related to PE/Sports Science

» **Fitness-centre manager**: employed mainly in commercial health clubs and gyms to manage the provision of physical fitness and lifestyle programmes.
» **Leisure-centre manager**: there are opportunities in both the public and private sectors for promoting and running leisure and recreation centres.

» **Lifestyle consultant**: employed mainly in the private sector to provide physical-fitness instruction and prescription of exercise/fitness programmes for individuals.

» **Outdoor-pursuits manager**: manages a centre offering instruction in outdoor activities to a wide range of people.

» **Secondary-school teacher/higher-education lecturer**: there are opportunities for teaching PE in tertiary and FE colleges as well as in maintained and independent schools. Lecturing in HE is also available.

» **Sports administrator**: works in a governing body or the Sports Council. The role may be similar to that of the sports-development officer (see below) but it is likely to have a greater emphasis on administrative and financial aspects.

» **Sports coach/instructor**: there are a few full-time posts in some sports. This work can also form part of the work of a sports-development officer or a recreation assistant in a sports centre.

» **Sports-development officer**: promotes various sports within the community, usually amongst particular target groups, or develops one sport on behalf of a local authority, governing body or professional association.

» **Sports therapist**: mainly concerned with the prevention and treatment of injury in sport and with improving and maintaining physical performance.

Graduate jobs in which a degree in PE/Sports Science could be useful

» **Armed forces**: the active nature of many of the jobs and the leadership role of officers can suit sports people.

» **Health-promotion specialist**: understanding nutrition and the relation of fitness to health is a useful background for a health-promotion specialist.

» **Journalism**: familiarity with sports is obviously an asset if you want to be a journalist specialising in reporting and writing about sport.

» **Marketing**: the sports equipment and leisurewear industries could well value your knowledge of sport and exercise.

» **Physiotherapist**: this would be good preparation for a career in sports therapy but the training would take at least two further years after your degree.

» **Police officer**: this challenging job could suit sports management/ science graduates for reasons similar to those given for the armed services.

Further information
British Association of Sport and Exercise Sciences (BASES) –
www.bases.org.uk
Sport England – www.sportengland.org
UK Sport – www.uksport.gov.uk

Physics

The study of Physics will help you to understand how the physical world works, and will prove useful if you are considering a career in engineering, electronics, computing and many others. This course will help you establish links between theory and experiment, and will also help you:

» Learn how scientific work is evaluated, published and verified by the scientific community
» Gain an understanding of how physics has changed over time and how it is used in the modern world
» Explore the properties of motion, nuclear physics, energy transfer and electricity
» Develop a better awareness of how advances in science and technology affect the world.

Main elements of the course
For an exact definition of the AS and A2 syllabus you will be studying, you should consult your school, college or the exam board itself. The following outline is roughly based on the Edexcel syllabus.

Unit 1: mechanics and radioactivity
Forces, vectors and motion; graphs, energy, power and efficiency; Newton's laws, moments and couples; momentum and impulse; radioactivity – types and detection; radioactivity – the nucleus; atomic and sub-atomic scattering.

Unit 2: electricity and thermal physics
Electrical properties; more advanced concepts; applied heat; the gas laws; kinetic theory; an introduction to thermodynamics; heat engines.

Unit 3: topics
Students can choose one of the following four topics to study:
astrophysics; solid materials; nuclear and particle physics; medical
physics.

Unit 4: waves and our universe
Motion in a circle; simple harmonic motion, SHM; waves and
interference; light (1); light (2); introduction to quantum physics; atomic
models; doppler, red shift and the creation of time.

Unit 5: forces and fields
Electrical fields (1); electrical fields (2); gravity fields; magnetic fields;
introduction to capacitance; inductance (1); inductance (2).

Unit 6: synthesis
This is a synoptic module where students draw on all the knowledge
gained from the different modules so far.

AS students complete modules one to three, A2 students complete all six
modules. This subject is also offered at AEA level by CCEA exam board.

How is A level Physics taught and assessed?
Students will need a GCSE in Physics to enrol in this subject, unless they
have very good grades in Mathematics and related subjects such as
Design and Technology. There is a lot of classroom work as well as
practical work in the lab, carrying out experiments. Assessment is by a
combination of written exams and assessed practical work. There is
usually no coursework component in A level Physics, so think twice before
choosing this subject if exams are not your strength!

Choosing other A level subjects to go with Physics
There is a lot of mathematics involved in A level Physics, so studying
Mathematics at A level is a big help, and more often than not you will
need Mathematics A level to study Physics at degree level. Other subjects
that go well with Physics include Engineering (Applied A level), Design and
Technology, Chemistry and ICT/Computing.

Physics at higher-education level
Physics at degree level has been around for a very long time and is well
established in many universities. Students usually have the option of
studying specific types of physics (eg Astrophysics) or they can choose
courses such as Applied Physics or Pure Physics.

A degree in Physics

Most Physics degrees have compulsory options in the first and second years with some flexibility later on. Modules of a Physics course could include:

» Classical mechanics and special relativity
» Nuclear physics
» Introductory quantum mechanics
» Electromagnetism
» Astrophysics
» Computational physics
» Radiation physics
» Introduction to plasma physics
» Statistical mechanics.

Combining Physics with other degree subjects

Popular combinations include: Physics and Mathematics, Physics and Management, Physics and Computer Science, Physics and Philosophy.

Foundation degrees and HNDs

There is an HND in Applied Physics and one or two Foundation degrees in Physics. Search at www.ucas.com.

Physics and your future career

Non-graduate jobs

It's hard to get a job that directly uses physics without at least an undergraduate degree in the subject. A job as a trainee lab technician is possible. In terms of non-science jobs, there will be opportunities in the commercial sector as long as you demonstrate the skills you've developed from the course, such as problem solving, numeracy, manual dexterity and logical thinking.

Graduate jobs related to Physics

» **Electronics engineer**: develops and designs an electronic product, process or device from the initial brief, through a tested prototype, to manufacture.
» **Geoscientist**: collects, analyses and appraises physical data about the earth in order to discover commercially exploitable mineral and hydrocarbon reserves.
» **Materials engineer**: works on the manufacture, development and use of a wide range of materials, eg glass and ceramics, metals, polymers.

» **Medical physicist**: provides scientific support to medical staff in the accurate, effective and safe diagnosis and treatment of patients.
» **Meteorologist**: interprets observations from the land surface, oceans and from the upper atmosphere to forecast weather both short and long term, eg the results of global warming.
» **Research scientist**: organises and carries out systematic investigations into physical properties, behaviour and phenomena with the aim of introducing, developing or improving products or processes.
» **Scientific laboratory technician**: assists scientists and others who are engaged in research, development, analysis or scientific investigations by carrying out a variety of technical and experimental tasks.
» **Secondary-school teacher**: teaches Physics and/or Balanced Science. A Postgraduate Certificate in Education (PGCE) is necessary for teaching posts in state schools.

Graduate jobs in which a degree in Physics could be useful

» **Forensic scientist**: investigates scientific aspects of crime, fires and accidents.
» **Scientific journalist**: researches, writes and edits scientific news articles and features.
» **Systems analyst**: analyses the requirements of systems in both a business and technical context and determines the optimum solutions.
» **Technical author**: designs and writes documentation which communicates technical information.
» **Technical sales engineer**: provides the major link between the company producing technical goods and services and its customers, negotiating sales, orders, price and quality.

Further information
Duncan, T, *Advanced Physics*, John Murray Books
Institute of Physics – www.iop.org
Physics and Astronomy online reference – www.physlink.com

Psychology

The study of Psychology will help you understand your own behaviour as well as that of other people. The course also looks at topical issues, such as stress, eyewitness testimony and eating disorders, which can be better understood and managed using psychological methods. A level Psychology will also help you learn about various different research methods and how to present results and theories as well as giving you an understanding of how a knowledge of psychology can be useful in everyday life. Students of this course develop the ability to critically analyse the nature and source of psychological theories and find out how to design and report psychological investigations and to interpret their results.

Main elements of the course
For an exact definition of the AS and A2 syllabus you will be studying, you should consult your school, college or the exam board itself. The following outline is roughly based on the AQA specification.

Unit 1: cognitive and developmental psychology
Part 1: cognitive psychology – human memory

Part 2: developmental psychology – attachments and developments

Unit 2: physiological psychology and individual differences
Part 1: physiological psychology – stress

Part 2: individual differences – abnormality

Unit 3: social psychology and research methods
Part 1: social psychology – social influence

Part 2: research methods

Unit 4: social, physiological, cognitive and developmental psychology
Part 1: social psychology

Part 2: physiological psychology

Part 3: cognitive psychology

Part 4: developmental psychology

Unit 5: individual differences and perspectives
Part 1: individual differences – issues in the classification and diagnosis of psychological abnormality; psychopathology; treating mental disorders

Part 2: perspectives – issues and debates; different approaches to psychology

Unit 6: coursework
Creating a project brief and analysing your collected data. Report writing.

AS students complete modules one to three; A2 students complete all six modules. This course is also offered at AEA level by AQA.

How is A level Psychology taught and assessed?
There is no need to have any prior knowledge of this subject to take it at A level. All you need is an interest in human behaviour and how the human mind works and at least a semi-scientific turn of mind. There is a lot of classroom work and taking notes about theories, but some practical experiments are also carried out. You also spend a long time learning how to carry out a psychological experiment and how to research effectively and correctly.

Choosing other A level subjects to go with Psychology
If you want to do a degree in Psychology then it doesn't usually matter which subjects you do alongside it. However, some universities may prefer you to have studied the sciences, or at least Biology. That said, Psychology also goes well with subjects such as Law, English, Philosophy and Business Studies.

Psychology at higher-education level

Psychology is offered at many universities and colleges. Like many subjects, it's possible to specialise in a type of Psychology, such as development psychology. What is important, if you want to be a professional psychologist later on, is that your undergraduate degree must be accredited by the British Psychological Society (BPS).

A degree in Psychology?

As with most courses, there are some core modules and some optional ones. Some sample modules of a university degree course might include:

» Statistical methods
» Biological psychology
» Sensation and perception
» Cognitive neuroscience
» Psychology of religion.

Combining Psychology with other degree subjects

Subjects often studied alongside Psychology include: Mathematics, Computing/ICT, Philosophy, Physics, English and Religious Studies.

Foundation degrees and HNDs

There are a few Psychology-related Foundation degrees available but they usually focus on one particular area, such as Psychology and Crime. There are HNDs specifically in Psychology but some students may be interested in the HNDs in Applied Biology or Health and Social Care, which have some overlap with Psychology.

Psychology and your future career

Non-graduate jobs

Psychology gives you many useful skills such as the ability to research, analyse data, think logically and communicate effectively. These skills will be sought after in most sectors, including health, business and other areas of the public sector. If you want to work in psychology, then further study is usually required.

Graduate jobs related to Psychology

For all the following careers except counselling, teaching and HE lecturing, a first degree in Psychology or alternative graduate conversion qualification, accredited by the British Psychological Society (BPS), is essential in order to enter further training and work.

» **Clinical psychologist**: applies psychology to the assessment and treatment of patients and clients in health-care settings and conducts research in mental and physical illness.
» **Counsellor**: helps people solve problems, cope with distress and improve wellbeing. Works with clients of all ages and in a variety of settings, including health, education and the workplace.
» **Educational psychologist**: applies psychology to the learning difficulties of children and young people and advises parents, teachers and schools.
» **Forensic psychologist**: applies psychology to criminological and legal issues including the assessment and treatment of offenders; may have trained in criminological or clinical psychology.
» **Health psychologist**: applies knowledge and understanding of behaviour to finding ways of improving the quality of health care and the standard of health in the general population.
» **Higher-education lecturer**: involved in teaching Psychology in colleges and higher-education institutions.
» **Occupational psychologist**: applies psychology to people at work and organisations including selection and assessment, training, work design and organisational change.

Graduate jobs in which a degree in Psychology could be useful

» **Market-research executive**: provides systematically acquired information on what people buy, want, do or think and explores the reasons why.
» **Personnel officer**: advises on and implements policies relating to the use of human resources, including employee planning, recruitment, training and welfare.
» **Psychotherapist**: develops a skilled relationship with clients in order to explore the underlying causes of their emotional conflicts or behavioural difficulties.
» **School teacher**: at secondary level, teaching social science, science or appropriate national curriculum subject.
» **Social researcher**: analyses the impact and expenditure implications of proposed policy changes and monitors the effects of change.
» **Social worker**: assisting and advising clients with social problems. Also specialisation as psychiatric social worker.
» **Speech-and-language therapist**: assesses, diagnoses and treats adults and children who suffer from disorders of voice, speech or language.

Further information
British Psychological Society – www.bps.org.uk
Gross, Richard, *The Psychology of Mind and Behaviour*, Hodder Arnold

Religious Studies

A level Religious Studies is for students of any religious persuasion or none. It considers the fundamental questions of human existence, examining issues such as the interaction between religion and science, as well as exploring religious experience and philosophical aspects of religious belief. In addition, you will be able to practise textual criticism skills developed by studying religious texts. You will also get a better understanding of world religions.

Main elements of the course
All exam boards offer this subject and the content is very similar among all five of them. The following outline is based largely on the OCR specification.

- Foundation for the study of religion
- Philosophy of religion
- Religious ethics
- Jewish scriptures
- New Testament (either the Gospels or the early Church)
- Developments in Christian thought
- Eastern religions: either Buddhism or Hinduism
- Islam
- Judaism.

Students going for AS study three units from the above themes, whereas A2 students complete six modules. This subject is also offered at Applied level by Edexcel.

How is A level Religious Studies taught and assessed?
Teaching is mainly classroom-based learning and discussion but there may be visits to sites of religious interest. Assessment is by a combination of written exams and possibly coursework or an extended essay.

Choosing other A level subjects to go with Religious Studies
A levels that go well with this subject include English Literature, History, Psychology, Philosophy and Latin or Greek.

Religious Studies at higher-education level
There are many opportunities to study this subject at a higher level and a degree in this subject might be called Religious Studies, Theology or Divinity.

A degree in Religious Studies
A degree in this subject would go into much more depth than at A level as well as being much broader in its scope in terms of the kind of religions and religious sects studied. A sample of units that you might study during a degree programme might include:

» Islam's beginnings
» Jewish thought and practice
» Anthropology of religion
» Does God exist?
» Moral theory and religion
» The problem of evil
» Islamic mysticism
» Theories of religion
» Religion and the Enlightenment.

Combining Religious Studies with other subjects
This subject could be combined with most humanities subjects and common combinations include: Theology and Religious Studies, History and Religious Studies, English Literature and Religious Studies, and Classics and Religious Studies.

Foundation degrees and HNDs
There are some Foundation degrees related to Religious Studies but they tend to be aiming for a specific vocation, eg Religious Studies and Ministry. There are no HNDs in Religious Studies.

Religious Studies and your future career

Non-graduate jobs
This is a sound A level that will enable you, along with your other subjects, to get junior positions in many areas of business, the public sector and the not-for-profit sector. Jobs related to Religious Studies would be hard to find without a degree, but getting an administrative position in a religious-based non-governmental organisation (NGO) would be a possibility.

Graduate jobs related to Religious Studies
The most directly related job is a Minister of Religion, who teaches the religious beliefs specific to the faith, ministering to the spiritual and social needs of people in the local community. Information is usually available through the minister of your church or religious organisation. Other related jobs include:

» **Adult-education lecturer/tutor**: plans and provides a programme of learning activities for adults of all ages, backgrounds and academic levels, in line with the tutor's own expertise.
» **Higher-education lecturer**: involves teaching (undergraduate and postgraduate students), research (which may include work for agencies outside the university) and administration.
» **Secondary-school teacher**: involves teaching Religious Studies and Theology in schools or colleges.

Graduate jobs in which a degree in Religious Studies could be useful

» **Charity officer**: promotes the work of the charity, being responsible for fund-raising, arranging recruitment, training and supervision of paid and voluntary staff, devising and managing the administrative systems, including the accounts.
» **Counsellor**: concerned with counselling people with personal problems. Helps the client to explore, discover and clarify more effective ways of living.
» **Housing advisor**: offers advice and support to people who have housing difficulties.
» **Journalist**: researches and writes features for broadcasting on television or radio, or publishing in periodicals and newspapers. As a theology student you might be interested in the specialist field of religious publications.

Further information

Buddhist Society – www.thebuddhistsociety.org.uk
Burke, T P, *An Introduction to the Major Religions*, Blackwell, 1995
Council of Christians and Jews – www.ccj.org.uk
Hinduism – www.comparative-religion.com/hinduism
Islamic Foundation – www.islamic-foundation.org.uk
National Society for Promoting Religious Education – www.natsoc.org.uk

Science, Applied

Applied Science is for students who want to learn about how science is applied in real, practical ways. This may be in commerce, in industry, in research or any other way that is practical or that affects people's lives. It is also for students who want to pursue specific scientific careers such as laboratory work. This subject will also develop your skills in ICT, numeracy, logical thinking and problem solving.

Main elements of the course

The exam boards that offer this subject cover very similar content. There are four possible routes for gaining an award in this subject: AS single award (three units); AS double award (six units); A level single award (six units); and A level double award (12 units).

» Unit 1: investigating science at work
» Unit 2: energy transfer systems
» Unit 3: finding out about substances
» Unit 4: food science and technology
» Unit 5: choosing and using materials
» Unit 6: synthesising organic compounds
» Unit 7: planning and carrying out a scientific investigation
» Unit 8: medical physics
» Unit 9: sports science
» Unit 10: physics of performance effects
» Unit 11: controlling chemical processes
» Unit 12: the actions and development of medicines
» Unit 13: colour chemistry
» Unit 14: the healthy body

■ Unit 15: the role of the pathology service
■ Unit 16: ecology, conservation and recycling.

How is Applied Science taught and assessed?

Students need to have reached a good standard in at least one GCSE science subject before taking this course. There is a lot of lab work, calculations and practical tasks. Sometimes visits are arranged to places of scientific interest (eg a chemical plant). Assessment is by a combination of written exams and portfolio of evidence.

Choosing other subjects to go with Applied Science

Other science subjects at A level would obviously go well, but ensure there is not too much overlap – university admissions tutors may not recognise your subjects as separate and therefore your points tally would be lower. Other subjects that might go well include Business, Environmental Science, Computing/ICT and Mathematics. If you want to study a particular science at university, you should study that subject at A level.

Science at higher-education level

There are some science-based degree courses for which Applied Science would count as a qualifying subject. Degrees such as Environmental Science, Biomedical Science, Health Science, Food Science, Sports Science and Forensic Science would fit into this category.

A degree in science?

The nature of the course will dictate the kind of modules studied but whatever the course there will usually be some compulsory modules in the first year and some specialised options in the last two years.

Combining science with other degree subjects

Science-related degrees are often combined with a whole range of subjects at university level. But the most common subjects that are studied jointly with a science include: Mathematics, ICT/Computing, Philosophy, Business/Management and sometimes a modern language.

Foundation degrees and HNDs

There are many different science Foundation courses available, and they tend to specialise in particular areas such as animal science or bioscience. HNDs are available in Applied Biology, Applied Chemistry, Applied Physics and Biomedical Science.

Science and your future career

Applied Science can set you up for particular career pathways in science such as working in scientific analysis, the environment, manufacturing, healthcare and electronics. In many cases, further study is required to work in scientific roles. Nevertheless, A level Science is still a good subject to prepare you for entry-level jobs in many sectors of work, including non-science areas such as commerce and the public sector.

Degree options for science graduates really depend on the particular course studied. Look under the career options section for the A level science subjects in this guide and you will see that there are many possible choices for science graduates.

Further information

Institute of Biology – www.iob.org
Forensic Science Society – www.forensic-science-society.org.uk
Institute of Biomedical Sciences – www.ibms.org
Institute of Physics – www.iop.org
NHS Careers – www.nhscareers.nhs.uk
Royal Society of Chemistry – www.chemsoc.org

Sociology

Sociology is the scientific study of society. It is about all kinds of social relationships that people share with each other; in their families, in their schools and in work. The A level course concentrates on a choice of family, the mass media, health and welfare policy, education, work and training and the study of the law and crime. As an A level sociologist, you will learn some of the methods used by sociologists and apply your knowledge to the study of a topic of your own choice to produce an individual piece of research for examination.

Main elements of the course
For an exact definition of the AS and A2 syllabus you will be studying, you should consult your school, college or the exam board itself. The following outline is based largely on the AQA syllabus.

» Module 1: families, households and health
» Module 2: education; wealth; poverty and welfare
» Module 3: sociological methods – the main methods used by sociologists, and their relationship to theory
» Module 4: power and politics; religion
» Module 5: theory and methods – an extension of Module 3, which includes issues such as: science; values and objectivity; post-modernity
» Module 6: crime and deviance.

Students who intend to complete the full AS and A2 course complete all six modules. Those going only for the AS complete modules one to three.

How is A level Sociology taught and assessed?

There is a lot of reading and writing in this subject and much
consideration of contemporary political and social issues. No prior
knowledge is needed, but an interest in the issues is important. You may
look at government policies, newspaper reports, films and social
documentaries to bolster your knowledge. Assessment is by a
combination of coursework and written exams.

Choosing other A level subjects to go with Sociology

This could be combined with arts or science subjects. Social Policy,
Politics/Government, Health and Social Care, and Economics would all go
well. Always be careful there isn't too much of an overlap between your
A level subjects.

Sociology at higher-education level

Sociology at a higher level will go into much more depth than was
possible at A level and you will develop many more critical approaches
with which to analyse the issues. Often Sociology is associated with Social
Policy at a departmental level in universities, even though they are
different subjects. Institutions do not normally require A level Social Policy
or Sociology to study the subject at degree level.

A degree in Sociology?

There are many different kinds of degree in this area. As well as Social
Policy and Sociology, universities sometimes offer a Social Science
degree, which covers both of these subjects and a bit more! Some of the
modules you might find on a three-year Sociology BA include:

» Sociological analysis of contemporary society
» Sociological thinking
» Deviance, crime and social control
» Stigma deviance and society
» Identity, difference and inequalities
» Introduction to race and ethnicity
» Research methods
» Key debates in sociology.

Combining Sociology with other degree subjects

This subject obviously goes well with Social Policy, but other possible
complementary subjects include: Politics, Economics, Philosophy,
Geography, English and History.

Foundation degrees and HNDs

There are some related Foundation degrees such as Social Science, but they tend to focus on specific aspects of Social Policy or Sociology such as Criminology. There are no HNDs currently on offer in this area, although HNDs in Social Science, Social Science and Management, and Social Care are available.

Sociology and your future career

Non-graduate jobs

This is a sound A level that, along with your other subjects, will enable you to get a junior position in many areas of business, the public sector and the not-for-profit sector. Jobs in sociology would be hard to find without a degree, but getting an administrative position in social services, the prison service or in a non-governmental organisation (NGO) would be a possibility.

Graduate jobs related to Sociology

- » **Education, teaching and lecturing**: this can be at secondary level, where a PGCE is required, or in further or higher education.
- » **Probation officer**: provides a social-work service to all the courts. Work involves the supervision of offenders in the community, the care of offenders in custody and the aftercare of released offenders.
- » **Social/community work**: this includes social work and community work, careers and educational guidance and counselling roles.
- » **Social research**: this could mean working for a local authority, charity/campaign organisation, trade union, political party or as a parliamentary research assistant at Westminster.
- » **Social worker**: supports people who need help or protection. Work is done with children and families but also with those coping with issues such as homelessness, addictions and mental health problems.

Graduate jobs in which a degree in Sociology could be useful

- » **Counsellor**: works with individuals and sometimes with groups, in confidence, to explore dissatisfaction or distress. A counsellor will aim to enable someone to overcome personal difficulties and facilitate change.
- » **Housing manager**: develops, supplies and manages housing for local authorities and housing associations.
- » **Prison governor**: plans, organises and co-ordinates, in accordance with Home-Office policies, the activities and resources necessary for the efficient running of a prison.

» **Welfare-rights adviser**: concerned with giving information and advice to members of the public on matters that are usually of a legal or financial nature and that affect the individual's rights and basic welfare.

Further information
Social Work Careers – www.socialworkcareers.co.uk
Sociology revision website – www.sociologystuff.com
Sociology website – www.sociology.org.uk

Travel and Tourism (Applied A level)

The global travel and tourism industry is still booming. This means the demand for well-qualified staff is high. As a student of this course, you will improve your knowledge, understanding and skills related to the vocational area of travel and tourism. It will also give you a good platform from which to study the subject further. As well as giving you a good background in this area, this subject also allows you to focus on particular career areas such as marketing, customer service, worldwide travel destinations and tourism development, and it will provide an appreciation of the wider travel and tourism environment.

Main elements of the course

The exam boards offering this course cover very similar ground in terms of content. The main variations are in terms of module names and how the options are organised. For an exact definition of the AS and A2 syllabus you will be studying, you should consult your school, college or the exam board itself. The following outline is based largely on the OCR syllabus.

- Unit 1: introducing travel and tourism
- Unit 2: customer service in travel and tourism
- Unit 3: travel destinations
- Unit 4: international travel
- Unit 5: tourist attractions
- Unit 6: organising travel
- Unit 7: hospitality
- Unit 8: working overseas
- Unit 9: tourism development
- Unit 10: event management

- Unit 11: the guided tour
- Unit 12: ecotourism
- Unit 13: adventure tourism
- Unit 14: culture tourism
- Unit 15: marketing in travel and tourism
- Unit 16: human resources in travel and tourism.

This course is available as a single or double award, at both AS level and A level.

How is A level Travel and Tourism taught and assessed?

You need no prior knowledge of this subject to take the course, but an interest in the topic as well as career motivation in this area are advantages. As well as classroom work, students may visit different travel and tourism organisations, and do lots of independent research about the sector. Assessment is by a combination of externally set and marked written exams and internally assessed portfolios of evidence.

Choosing other A level subjects to go with Travel and Tourism

This subject goes well with other Applied subjects such as Leisure Studies and Applied Business. (Check in case there may be too much overlap and exam boards may not permit the combination.) Equally, it would go well with GCE A levels in Business, Accounting or a foreign language.

Travel and Tourism at higher-education level

There are different types of course in this area. There are a few degree courses, such as Travel and Tourism Management, but there are also many options at Foundation degree and HND level. Some degree courses are sandwich courses, meaning that students work for a year in the travel and tourism industry at some point during their course. Some courses offer a year-abroad option. You don't necessarily need to have studied this subject previously to be accepted onto a degree course.

A degree in Travel and Tourism?

Modules of a BA (Hons) degree in this subject might include the following:

- Tourism today
- Incoming and domestic tourism
- Travel trade and IATA studies

» Organisational studies
» World geography or a language (French, German or Spanish)
» Marketing and accounting
» Visitor-attraction studies
» Travel-agency operations
» Global-tourism issues
» E-tourism
» Adventure tourism.

Combining Travel and Tourism with other degree subjects

This subject goes very well with a modern foreign language as well as subjects such as Business/Management, Accounting, Geography and Computing/ICT.

Foundation degrees and HNDs

There are many Travel and Tourism Foundation degrees as well as some related to specific areas of the sector. Edexcel offers an HND in Travel and Tourism Management.

Travel, Tourism and your future career

Non-graduate jobs

This sector is always crying out for people so it's a bit easier for students to get jobs straight after A levels. Trainee positions do exist with travel companies, agencies and tour operators as well as with some airlines.

Graduate jobs related to Travel and Tourism

» **Holiday rep**: employed in resorts to look after holidaymakers, includes children's reps and administrators. Work is hard and demanding, usually working on rota systems.
» **Tour manager**: travels with groups of holidaymakers on package tours at home and overseas.
» **Tourism officer**: develops and promotes a quality tourism product which will attract visitors and produce significant economic benefits for a country or region.
» **Tourist-information-centre manager**: provides information to visitors to the area and sells guidebooks, maps and products.
» **Travel agent**: acts as a link between the client and tour operator. Responsible for advising customers and selling travel services.

Graduate jobs in which a degree in Travel and Tourism could be useful

» **Arts administrator**: responsible for managing the theatre/gallery, etc, managing financial resources, marketing and attracting sponsorship to support the arts.
» **Events organiser**: identifies potential business, researches, writes, plans and runs all aspects of conferences or exhibitions on behalf of a client or own organisation.
» **Hotel manager**: manages hotel, restaurant, etc whilst promoting facilities and services, organising special events and recruiting staff.
» **Public-relations officer**: writes press releases, produces publicity brochures and promotional literature (may work in conjunction with marketing department), produces customer/staff newspapers and magazines.

Further information
Association of British Travel Agents (ABTA) www.abta.com
Institute of Travel and Tourism – www.itt.co.uk
Travel Industry Jobs website – www.travelindustryjobs.co.uk

PART THREE: EXAMS AND BEYOND

Making a success of your studies: Revision tips

In this section you will:
- *find out how you learn effectively*
- *learn how to prepare effectively for exams*
- *discover how exam boards assess students' work*
- *think about ways of improving your exam technique.*

How do you learn best?

Having made the choices about *what* you're going to study, your main focus will probably shift to *how* you're going to study. There are many different ways of studying and revising and you need to find methods that work best for you. In reality, your teacher or tutor will use different methods to allow for the fact that people learn in different ways. But do you know how you learn best? Do you know why some activities appeal to you and some don't?

There has been lots of research about this and lots of theories developed but a very simple one is shown in the table overleaf. Are you someone who learns best by seeing or visualising things (a visual learner)? Or do you remember by what you hear (auditory)? Or are you a hands-on practical learner, someone who needs to feel and touch things (kinesthetic)? Look at the questions on the left and put a tick or a cross next to the one(s) that apply to you most (more than one statement may be true for you for each question). Then total up your ticks at the end.

	Visual	Auditory	Kinesthetic/tactile
When I try to spell a word I ...	try to see to see the word in my mind's eye	say the word aloud to see what it sounds like	write the word down to find out if it feels right
When I'm having a conversation I ...	don't like listening for too long. I tend to use words such as 'see', 'picture', 'imagine'	enjoy listening but am impatient to talk. I use words such as 'hear' and 'it sounds like'	gesture and use expressive movements. I use words such as 'feel', 'touch' and 'hold'
When I'm concentrating I become distracted by ...	untidiness or movements	sounds or noises	activity around me
When I've met someone once before I ...	can't remember their name but remember their face	can't remember what they look like, but remember their name and what was talked about	remember best what we did together
When I'm trying to contact someone I ...	prefer to see them face to face	prefer to use the telephone	prefer to talk to them while walking or engaging in an activity
When I read a book I ...	enjoy descriptive scenes and vivid imagery	enjoy the dialogue and conversation between characters	prefer action stories (or don't enjoy it because I'm not a keen reader)
When I'm learning things, I ...	like to see demonstrations, diagrams, slides or posters	prefer verbal instructions or talking about it with someone else	prefer to try and do it myself if possible and 'get stuck in'
Totals			

Adapted from Colin Rose, *Accelerated Learning*, Accelerated Learning Systems Ltd, 1985

Some people have a very strong preference for one way of doing things; others are more of a mixture of all three. Whatever your preference, it's important to think about this (as well as any other insights about the way you take in and remember information best) when you're thinking about the best ways to study and revise. For instance, look at the following examples, which show how you can use this information to improve your learning ability.

Situation: You can't understand something your teacher is trying to explain.
Options: Ask politely if he or she could write it down or put it in a diagram, or try to draw it yourself.

Situation: You can't seem to remember much by looking over your revision notes.
Options: Record your notes on tape and listen to them, or get someone to test you and make a game out of it!

These are just two examples of how doing things in a different way can make it much easier for you to learn and therefore enjoy the subject.

Your strategy for success
As well as taking into account how your brain works best, there are lots of other practical things you can do to make studies as successful as possible. Success at this level really comes down to four things: being organised, understanding what the exam board wants, revision and assessment/exam technique. Let's look at each in turn.

Get organised!
As soon as you start school or college for your post-16 qualifications, you will be given a timetable. Unlike GCSE study, when all your time is accounted for at school, at this stage you will probably have periods where you don't have any lessons. You could build your own personal timetable into the official timetable, taking into account the following:

- Time for independent study or revision
- Time for socialising
- Time for part-time work (if you have to do it)
- Time doing nothing!

For each subject you are studying, your tutor will give you an idea of how much independent reading around the subject is required to get a good grade. Once you get this information, you will be able to build it into your timetable.

Other simple ways of staying organised include:

» Keeping a notebook of things to do so you don't forget them
» Not taking on too much work outside studies
» Getting into the habit of doing things straight away rather than leaving them (if possible)
» Keeping daily lists of things to do.

Effective note-taking is very important for study at this level. You might not have time to write down every single word your teacher says on a subject, but try to get into the habit of recording at least the key information. Remember, too, that you will have to do a lot of note-taking at home when you are reading around the subject.

Understanding what the exam boards want
How A levels, AS levels and equivalents are assessed does vary from subject to subject, but there are many elements that are common to all of them. They are outlined below.

Synoptic modules
Most subjects are broken down into specific units. As a student who has mastered their subject, you don't just have to do well in each unit, but you need to show that you can make connections across all the units that you've learned. This, in essence, is what synoptic modules are all about. Synoptic modules are sometimes only a requirement of the A2 part of the course, however, and not part of the AS requirement. So, even if you're not doing the exam for a synoptic module, it's always a good idea to make references to other areas of the subject where possible. This shows a breadth of knowledge.

Skills
These days syllabuses are called specifications. This is because you are being assessed on the skills you've developed as well as the knowledge you've acquired. Both examinations and coursework test a number of subject-based skills, such as planning and experimental skills in science and reading and listening in modern languages.

Spiritual, moral, ethical, cultural and other issues
Students are also supposed to show an awareness of these issues in relation to what they are studying. Mentioning these issues, where relevant, in coursework and exams will probably help your cause.

Coursework
As well as written exams, many subjects have an element of coursework assessment; a large amount in some subjects, very little in others.

Examiners look for the same kinds of skills that they would in written exams, although different criteria may be applied to some subjects. Coursework is marked by your class teacher and a sample of the work is sent to the exam board to be moderated. Sometimes this is marked down by the moderator, so bear in mind that the mark that your teacher gives you is not necessarily the final mark!

Grading and grade boundaries

Grade boundaries are set each year when all the marks are in, and they vary from year to year. In reality, what this means is that someone may get a grade A one year with a certain standard of work, and the following year another person might get a grade B for the same standard of work. It seems unfair, but that's the way the system works. Having said that, the descriptions of grades are pretty much standard, and it's quite clear what's a very good standard and what's of an average standard. Take this example below, which is a definition of grades, A, C and E in relation to A level Law (AQA Exam board):

- **Grade A**: candidates are able to recall a substantial body of relevant information and present a well-structured response to the question, identifying a range of issues. They are able consistently to integrate descriptive and evaluative material, make connections where appropriate, demonstrate strong analytical and problem-solving skills and conduct a sound, coherent and relevant argument, supported appropriately.
- **Grade C**: candidates recall a sound body of information and are able to relate it to issues raised by the questions. They demonstrate some analytical and problem-solving skills, make connections and present a sound argument with some use of authority or other evidence.
- **Grade E**: candidates either provide generally accurate accounts of some relevant, descriptive material and/or identify issues raised by the question, identify connections and offer a basic evaluation, drawing simple conclusions.

Applied A level subjects

In general, applied subjects contain a much lower element of written exams. Instead, emphasis is placed on building up a portfolio of evidence, which could include a case study, a report, practical work (eg something you've created) or anything else. These portfolios are often internally assessed and externally moderated, but some elements of the applied courses are also assessed by external examiners.

Revision technique

There are many ways to revise, and different things work for different people. Look at the following list of tips and see what works best for you.

» Just as you created a timetable for study, you should also draw up a revision timetable. Work out when your exams are and calculate how much time you need to revise thoroughly for each one. Don't leave this too late or too near to the start of your exams.
» Know where your exams are and when they start, how long they are and what equipment you are allowed to take in (calculators, etc) and what you are not allowed to take in (mobiles phones, etc).
» Make sure you have one weekend day when you don't do revision or think about exams – you'll come back to your work feeling refreshed.
» Start by putting everything you need to know on a piece of paper. Then, as you keep revising it, reduce it to the key points and the stuff you can't remember. Gradually, you should be able to get all your revision key points onto a postcard!
» Some people (auditory people!) revise well by listening, so they could 'talk' their revision onto cassette tapes and then listen to these while lying in bed, while travelling in a car or walking to the shops (on a personal stereo).
» Having a good diet and getting enough rest as well as some regular exercise helps keep you energised, focused and optimistic. Have an early night before exams.
» On the morning of the exam, have a good breakfast, stay calm and allow plenty of time to get to the exam. Remember that you can only do your best.

Assessment/exam technique

» Before the exams, have a look at the exam board's specification to see what is required to achieve the different grades. Look at any past papers to give you an idea of the types of question you may be facing.
» In terms of coursework assessment, before you hand in your work, make sure it meets the requirements outlined by your teacher – and on the exam board's website if you wish.
» During an exam, work out how much time you've got for each section of the paper and stick to your plan.
» If you have to write an essay during an exam, spend some time at the start of the exam coming up with a plan and structure for the essay. This will keep you on track.
» If you finish the exam early, go back and check over your work. You may not feel like doing this, but it could mean the difference between one grade and the next!

Further help

A–Z of Exam Survival, Trotman Publishing

BBC Learning site. Gives revision help not just for A levels and AS levels, but also Scottish Highers and Welsh Exams – www.bbc.co.uk/learning/subjects/schools.shtml

Examzone (a site hosted by Edexcel) – www.examzone.co.uk

The Student Room (online forum for students to share exam experiences, help with revision, etc) – www.thestudentroom.co.uk

End note: What next?

In this section you will:
» *find out a bit more about some of the options open to you after your Level 3 qualifications.*

Decisions, decisions! Once you've chosen your Level 3 qualifications, it won't be long before you have to think about what to do afterwards. Higher education is an obvious choice for many, but it's not the only thing on offer. Here are some of the options.

Higher/further education
There are a number of options, including:

» **Academic degree** such as Maths, Physics, English, History, a modern language and so on. These courses usually last three years, sometimes four. This is still the most popular option in terms of higher education and remains the gateway for many of the higher-salaried jobs. For more detailed information see the section on higher education options for each of the corresponding A level entries. You can also search for a course at www.ucas.com.
» **Vocational degree** such as Medicine, Engineering, Dentistry, Nursing and so on. These courses often take longer than three years and sometimes include on-the-job experience as part of the qualification.
» **Sandwich/industrial-degree** subjects such as Business Studies, Engineering, ICT/Computing, Retail Management and so on. These are courses that include a year's placement in a relevant industry.
» **Foundation degree**. These are offered in the whole range of subjects but are usually vocationally based and include work experience. They last two years and can be converted to a full degree. Search for them at www.ucas.com.

» **Higher National Diploma (HND)**. These are similar to Foundation degrees in that they tend to be vocationally based but can be converted to full degrees and can provide a gateway to further study. Unlike Foundation degrees, however, they receive more recognition from employers, partly because they have been around for much longer.

All of the above can be taken on a full-time or part-time basis and some subjects may be studied alone or jointly with other subjects (eg French with History).

Straight into employment

It's a fact that more and more jobs can only be accessed by those who've been through higher education. However, there are still many areas of work where it's possible to climb the ladder from a Level 3 qualification such as A levels, Scottish Highers or equivalents. These include:

» **Civil Service/local government**. As an A level/equivalent student, it's possible to get junior administrative positions in this sector and then work your way up.
» **Hospitality and catering**. Many hotels run their own training schemes for hotel managers, for which you don't necessarily need a degree. On-the-job experience is more important.
» **Journalism and the media**. Some local newspapers still take on school leavers and train them up. This is how many top journalists started in the profession.
» **Leisure and recreation**. Jobs in sports centres, in health and fitness clubs and as personal trainers are all possible without a degree.
» **Retail (some areas)**. Many organisations (such as the Arcadia Group) in this sector offer specific training schemes for Level 3-qualified students who don't want to go on to higher education.
» **Sales**. If you can sell, that's the main thing that counts. You don't need to have a degree.
» **Travel, tourism and the airline business**. It's possible to get started with an airline (maybe as a cabin-crew member) or in the travel business, which has specific schemes. An applied A level in Travel and Tourism might help.

These are just some of the work-related options, but there are many more. Speak to your school careers advisor, if you have one, or your Connexions advisor for further guidance.

Taking time out before employment or further study

This is a very common option. It may be that you need some time to think before making your next move, it could be that you need a break from studying, or you might want to get some work experience before going on to further study. From the point of view of an employer or a university admissions department, it's not a problem at all, as long as you can show that you've done something worthwhile with the time. Some of the gap-year options include:

» Getting some work experience, perhaps in an area that you might move into later
» Travel abroad to broaden your horizons
» Do some charity/voluntary work overseas (such as VSO)
» Teach English abroad
» A combination of the above!

If you approach it in the right way, and don't spend the whole year lying on a beach somewhere, then taking a year out can really add to your skills, develop your maturity and generally make you more employable.

Whatever you decide to do, always try to focus on why you're doing it, where it's leading and whether you're going to enjoy it. With these three things in mind, you should make good decisions throughout your life. I wish you well.

How to find out more

Connexions website (lots of information about post-16 and post-18 choices) – www.connexions-direct.com
Edexcel website (where you can search for HNDs) – www.edexcel.org.uk
Gap-year website – www.yearoutgroup.org
UCAS website (where you can search for full degrees and Foundation degrees) – www.ucas.com